Introducing

Grammar

Edward Woods

Series Editors:
Ronald Carter and David Nunan

PENGUIN
ENGLISH

PENGUIN ENGLISH

Published by the Penguin Group
Penguin Books Ltd, 27 Wrights Lane, London W8 5TZ, England
Penguin Books USA Inc., 375 Hudson Street, New York, New York 10014, USA
Penguin Books Australia Ltd, Ringwood, Victoria, Australia
Penguin Books Canada Ltd, 10 Alcorn Avenue, Toronto, Ontario, Canada M4V 3B2
Penguin Books (NZ) Ltd, 182–190 Wairau Road, Auckland 10, New Zealand

Penguin Books Ltd, Registered Offices: Harmondsworth, Middlesex, England

First published 1995
1 3 5 7 9 10 8 6 4 2

Typeset by Datix International Limited, Bungay, Suffolk
Printed in England by Clays Ltd, St Ives plc
Filmset in 10/13 pt Monophoto Times

For Hannah, Lee & Marc

The insights provided by work in applied linguistics can be of genuine support to all teachers facing the many complex demands of language learning and teaching. The Penguin English *Introducing Applied Linguistics* series aims to provide short, clear and accessible guides to key topics – helping teachers to keep abreast of this rapidly developing field by explaining recent research and its relevance to common problems and concerns. The books are designed for practical use: they focus on recognizable classroom contexts, suggest problem-solving approaches, and include activities and questions for further study.

Introducing Applied Linguistics presumes an increasing convergence of interest among all English language teachers, and it aims to be relevant both to teachers of English as a second or foreign language and to teachers of English as a mother tongue. As the relationship between linguistics and language teaching continues to develop, so the need grows for books which introduce the field. This series has been developed to meet that need.

The words that appear in **bold** type are
explained in the glossary.

Penguin English
Introducing Grammar

Edward G. Woods is a Teaching Fellow at the Institute
for English Language Education at Lancaster University,
where he is the Area Co-ordinator for the Direct Language
Teaching programme and co-ordinator of the Summer
pre-sessional programme. Before coming to Lancaster he
was with International House and at the Freie Universitat
in Berlin. He has worked as a teacher and teacher trainer
in many parts of the world, including Iran, Italy, Japan
and Morocco. He has also run seminars and some con-
sultancies in many countries. In addition to grammar, he
has professional interests in using video in the classroom,
the roles of British Studies and ethnography, and classroom
action research. He is a co-author of *Using English Grammar* (1990) and *Using Basic English Grammar* (1992), both
published by Prentice Hall. He is a co-author of the course
Eurolingua, published originally by Migros (Switzerland),
and to be republished by Cornelsen (Germany).

Ronald Carter is Professor of Modern English Language
in the Department of English Studies at the University of
Nottingham. He is the author of many books on applied
linguistics and was the National Co-ordinator for the
LINC (Language in the National Curriculum) project
from 1989 to 1992.

David Nunan is Professor of Applied Linguistics and
Director of the English Centre at the University of Hong
Kong. He has worked as a TESOL teacher, teacher
educator, curriculum designer, and materals writer, and
consultant in Britain and overseas and is the author of
many books on applied linguistics and ELT.

Contents

Contents

Contents

Acknowledgements

I would like to thank the many people who in different ways have helped me in writing this book.

Nicki McLeod, Dr Pauline Rea-Dickins, Dr Alan Walton and John Williams for the ideas they provided. All the students who have practised the tasks and commented; and all the participants on teacher training courses, who have heard talks based on the ideas in this book and who by their questions and comments have helped me to refine those ideas.

I also have to thank Gareth Hughes and Maggy McNorton, who read the manuscript at various stages, for their sharp and perceptive comments and suggestions.

Esme Kitchin, the Resources Centre librarian at the Institute for English Language Education, for giving me easy access to the books and journals in the centre, and constantly drawing my attention to articles and papers I would otherwise have overlooked.

Finally, I must thank Mione Ieronymidis for the way she edited the manuscript and the useful, practical suggestions she made.

Without these people, I couldn't have written the book. They deserve all the credit. I alone am responsible for any failings.

The publishers make grateful acknowledgement to the following for permission to reproduce copyright material: *English Grammar Today* by G. Leech, M. Deuchar and R. Hoogenraad, Macmillan Press Ltd, 1982; *Teaching Grammar – a Guide for the National Curriculum* by R. Hudson, Basil Blackwell Ltd, 1992;

Acknowledgements

A Comprehensive Grammar of the English Language by R. Quirk, S. Greenbaum, G. Leech and J. Svartvik, Longman Group Ltd, 1985; *Collins Cobuild English Grammar*, © William Collins & Sons, 1990; *A Communicative Grammar of English* by G. Leech and J. Svartvik, Longman Group Ltd, 1975; *English as a Foreign Language* by R. A. Close, George Allen & Unwin, 1981; *Designing Tasks for the Communicative Classroom* by D. Nunan, Cambridge University Press, 1989; *Meaning and Form* by D. Bolinger, Longman Group Ltd, 1977; *Educational Linguistics* by M. Stubbs, Basil Blackwell Ltd, 1986; *Strategies* by B. Abbs, A. Ayton and I. Freebairn, Longman Group Ltd, 1975; *Streamline English* by B. Hartley and P. Viney, Oxford University Press, 1978, © Oxford University Press and reprinted by permission; *The New Cambridge English Course Students Book 1* by M. Swan and C. Walter, Cambridge University Press, 1990; *Second Language Learning and Language Teaching* by V. Cook, Edward Arnold, 1991; *The National Curriculum for English* by R. Carter, The British Council, 1991; *Teaching the 'General' Student* by C. Brumfit, from *Communication in the Classroom* by K. Johnson and K. Morrow (eds.), Longman Group Ltd, 1981; *Focus on the Language Learner* by E. Tarone and G. Yule, Oxford University Press, 1989, by permission of Oxford University Press; *Modern Foreign Languages Non-statutory Guidance*, National Curriculum Council, 1992; *The Lexical Syllabus* by D. Willis, William Collins & Sons, 1990, © William Collins & Sons, 1990; *On Understanding Grammar* by T. Givon, Academic Press, 1979; *The Communicative Syllabus* by J. Yalden, Pergamon Press, 1983; *Making Informed Decisions About the Role of Grammar in Language Teaching* by M. Celce-Murcia, T. E. S. O. L. Newsletter, vol. XIX, no. 1, 1985, reprinted by permission; *Self-study Grammar Practice: Learners Views and Preferences* by A. Fortune, E. L. T. Journal, vol. 46, no. 2, 1992, reprinted by permission of Oxford University Press; *The Communicative Approach to Language Teaching* by C. Brumfit and K. Johnson, Oxford University

Press, 1979, © Oxford University Press and reprinted by permission; *Towards Task-based Language Learning* by C. Candlin, from *Language Learning Tasks* by C. Candlin and D. Murphy, vol. 7, Lancaster Practical Papers in English Language Education, Prentice Hall, 1987; *Collins Cobuild English Course* by J. Willis and D. Willis, William Collins & Sons, 1988, © William Collins & Sons; *Neither history, nor polemic, but this is a fine romance* by D. Malcolm, The Guardian, 1982, © The Guardian; *Language Awareness: a Missing Link in Language Teacher Education?* by T. Wright and R. Bolitho, E. L. T. Journal, vol. 47, no. 4, 1993, reprinted by permission of Oxford University Press; *English Grammar Lessons* by M. Dean, Oxford University Press, 1993; *What the 'Good Language Learner' Can Teach Us* by J. Rubin, T. E. S. O. L. Quarterly, vol. 9, no. 1, 1975, reprinted by permission.

Every effort has been made to trace copyright holders in every case. The publishers would be interested to hear from any not acknowledged here.

For a full list of references, please see page 117.

Introduction

After several years in the wilderness, in both **L1** and **L2** teaching, grammar has been the subject of a renewal of interest in the last decade.

It would, however, be a mistake to go back to the situation that existed some two or three decades ago. Grammar became unfashionable for very good reasons. So while the apparent abandonment of it from the curriculum might have been wrong, we should consider carefully what role it plays in language and communication before we put it back there.

In the first part of this book, I have tried to show why I think grammar is an important part of communication and, therefore, why it is important in a language programme. In the second part, I have looked at its place in the curriculum and examined approaches to the syllabus, then considered a methodology and suggested some task types.

Most of my work has been done in the L2 classroom, but there are many similarities in the work done in grammar in the L1 classroom. The cognitive methodology, with its consciousness-raising tasks, applies to learners of both L1 and L2.

It has not been my intention to discuss each structure; rather, I hope that I have set out an approach which can be adapted to all situations.

1   What is grammar?

1.1   Definitions

As we shall see, the term 'grammar' can be defined in a number of different ways.

ACTIVITY

Before you start reading this chapter, write your own very brief definition of 'Grammar'. Then study the following and make any changes to your definition.

In *An English Grammar for the Use of Schools*, published by direction of the Commissioners of National Education in Ireland in 1856, grammar is described as:

that science which teaches the proper use of letters, syllables, words, and sentences; or which treats the principles and rules of spoken and written language.

The object of English Grammar is to teach those who use the English language to express their thoughts correctly, either in speaking or writing.

English Grammar is divided into four parts: namely, Orthography, Etymology, Syntax and Prosody.

Orthography treats of letters, and of the mode of combining them into syllables and words.

Etymology treats of the various classes of words and of the changes which they undergo.

Syntax treats of the connexion and arrangement of words in sentences.

Prosody treats of the proper manner of speaking and reading, and of the different kinds of verse.

1

Even earlier, in one of the letters to his son, which make up his *A Grammar of the English Language*, intended for the use of schools and of young persons in general, but more especially for the use of soldiers, sailors, apprentices and plough-boys, Cobbett (1819) had said:

Grammar, as I have observed to you before, teaches us how to make use of words; that is to say, it teaches us how to make use of them in a proper manner, as I used to teach you how to sow and plant the beds in the garden; for you have throwed about seeds and stuck in plants of some sort or other, in some way or other, without any teaching of mine: and so can any body, without rules or instructions, put masses of words on paper; but to be able to choose the words which ought to be placed, we must become acquainted with certain principles and rules; and these principles and rules constitute what is called Grammar. (Cobbett 1819)

The problem with trying to give a definition to the term 'grammar' is that different people mark different parameters. Some people even see grammar as one of the moral pillars of society. In Britain, one politician has sought to blame football hooliganism on poor grammar teaching in schools.

Looking at what some of the professionals involved with language say, i.e. language teachers and grammarians, we can still find problems in setting the parameters in linguistic terms. At times it can be included into any aspect of language analysis, including morphology, phonology, **discourse analysis**, **pragmatics**. All of these have come under the umbrella of 'grammar' at one time or another.

1.1.1 Grammarians

Leech *et al.* (1982) see grammar as a central component 'which relates phonology and semantics, or sound and meaning'. They

What is grammar?

modify that description to include 'writing systems', and see the
relationship of grammar as:

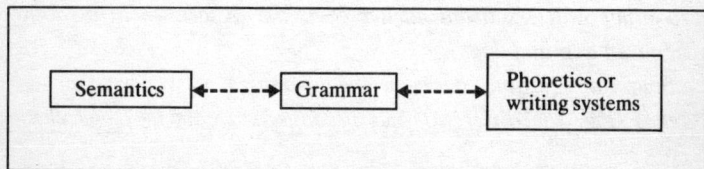

Semantics	←-----→	Grammar	←-----	Phonetics or writing systems

Huddleston (1988) says 'the two most basic units of grammar
are the word and the sentence, one subcomponent of grammar,
called morphology, deals with the forms of words, while the
other, called **syntax**, deals with the way words combine to form
sentences'.

ACTIVITY   *definition*

Hudson (1992) says that his 'conclusion ... is that there are
no natural boundaries around "grammar', so in principle I shall
allow the term to embrace any kind of information about
words'. However for the purpose of his book about teaching
grammar, he uses the term more narrowly. Consider his definition. What would you add to Hudson's list?

1a

It will refer to the following kinds of facts about words:
1. *about the classes to which they belong (e.g. 'noun');*
2. *about the structures of words that can be described in terms of
   notions like* **'suffix'** *(e.g. dogs = stem + suffix);*
3. *about the abstract distinctions that are sometimes signalled by
   these word structure differences (e.g. 'singular' versus 'plural');*
4. *about the abstract relations among words in sentences which I
   have called their 'grammatical function' (e.g. 'subject');*

3

5 *about the order in which words occur (e.g. 'TOO + adjective' precedes A);*
6 *about certain parts of word-meaning, when these can be related to other matters listed earlier (e.g. the difference in meaning between dog and dogs);*
7 *about the relations between the meanings of words in a sentence (e.g. the different roles of dogs and cats in Dogs chase cats);*
8 *about the 'informational' structures signalled for instance by differences in word order (e.g. the difference between I can't stand cats and Cats I can't stand);*
9 *about register differences between word-patterns (e.g. This is Dick Hudson here, used only on the telephone, versus the synonymous I'm Dick Hudson, which is used elsewhere).*
(Hudson 1922)

He goes on to admit that even with these limitations grammar is still a vast field.

1.1.2 Teachers

Ur (1988) says it '. . . may be roughly defined as the way a language manipulates and combines words (or bits of words) to form longer units of meaning', while Harmer's view is that it:

'is the way in which words change themselves and group together to make sentences. The grammar of a language is what happens to words when they become plural or negative, or what order is used when we make questions or join two clauses to make one sentence'. (Harmer 1987)

1.2 Types of grammar

The term 'Grammar' itself is used to mean many things. It can be a book like *A Comprehensive Grammar of the English Language*, which sets out rules for the language; it can be a school subject which teaches learners how to use their language correctly; or it can be an approach to analysing and describing language.

Sections 1.2.1–1.2.5 are some of the approaches to analysis and description of language which have influenced the teaching of grammar.

1.2.1 Prescriptive and descriptive grammar

Traditionally, grammar books such as those by Cobbett and the Commissioners of National Education in Ireland saw the correct use of language prescribed by a set of rules that were immutable. Early Grammars set down such rules, which allowed judgements to be made about a person's educated status. Such grammar books are considered to be 'prescriptive' grammars.

Grammar books written today, such as *A Comprehensive Grammar of the English Language*, (Quirk *et al.* 1985), or *Collins COBUILD English Grammar* (1990), are more concerned with looking at how language is actually used. Although some of the rules prescribed in the earlier grammar books still pertain, modern grammars describe the language in **use** and are known as 'descriptive' grammars.

Descriptive grammar books acknowledge that language is dynamic and, therefore, that how it is used is constantly changing – not in major ways, but slowly and almost imperceptibly L1 users of the language are making utterances or writing sentences which a generation before would have been considered incorrect.

For example, the prescribed rule is that '*a few* determines plural count nouns (*a few books*)' and '*a little* determines noncount nouns (*a little poetry*)' (Quirk *et al.* 1985). They then go on to explain the comparative and superlative forms (*few*fewer*fewest and little*less*least*). However, they then acknowledge that 'There is a tendency to use *less* (instead of *fewer*) and *least* (instead of *fewest*) also with count nouns'. They are describing the language as it is used.

The problem with such descriptive grammar books for learners of English as a Foreign language is that there is a time-lag between the awareness that such changes are occurring in the language and their acceptance as the proper use of the language. This is also the case with native speakers. Many people deplore some of the changes that are occurring in the language. Furthermore, there is often a time-lag between when something is accepted in the spoken language and when it is acceptable in the written language.

The problem for **EFL** learners is different from that for native speakers. The acceptance period is much shorter for native speakers and because of the media around them, they become aware when such changes have general acceptance. The L2 speaker does not have this luxury and has to rely on the rules set down in the grammar books. In this way, even descriptive grammar books can become prescriptive.

1.2.2 Traditional grammars

Grammar books such as Cobbett's and the Irish grammar have at their centre the syntax of the language. In teaching the syntactic organization of the sentence, they look at the different classes of words that make up the sentence, such as noun, verb, adjective, preposition, adverb, etc.

They focus on the sentence and consider the role and relationships of words in the sentence such as subject, object, etc. This organization of language helps to show the different clause types. Quirk *et al.* (1985) identify seven clause types, each associated with a set of verbs.

CLAUSE TYPES

	S(ubject)	V(erb)	O(bject(s))	C(omplement)	A(dverbial)
Type *SV*	Someone	was laughing			[1a]
Type *SVO*	My mother	enjoys	parties		[2a]
Type *SVC*	The country	became		totally independent	[3a]
Type *SVA*	I	have been			in the garden [4a]
Type *SVOO*	Mary	gave	the visitor a glass of milk		[5a]
Type *SVOC*	Most people	consider	these books	rather expensive	[6a]
Type *SVOA*	You	must put	all the toys		upstairs [7a]

(Quirk *et al.* 1985: 2.16)

Languages such as English are known as S–V–O languages because the unmarked order of the sentence is Subject–Verb–Object. Thus if we see three words such as <u>Man–See–Woman</u> without any other grammatical organization, we are most likely to conclude that it is a man who sees a woman, because of the order of the words.

Other languages have a different unmarked ordering. For example in Farsi and Japanese the order is S–O–V, and in Arabic it is V–S–O.

1.2.3 Phrase-structure grammar

Phrase-structure grammar developed the work done with traditional grammars and set out to show more graphically how words and phrases related to each other in a sentence.

Cook (1991) suggests that teachers had been using this directly in *substitution tables* since the 1920s. It was also used as the basis for many grammar lessons for L1 learners in the nineteen-forties and fifties.

SENTENCE					
NOUN PHRASE		VERB PHRASE			
		Verb		Noun phrase	
article	noun (pl)	verb stem	+ past	article	noun (pl)
the	boy -s	watch	-ed	the	game -s

1.2.4 Transformational-generative grammar

Chomsky's transformational-generative grammar essentially looks at syntax but it incorporates more than Phrase-structure grammar does, and includes both phonology and **semantics**. TGG is concerned with the universal characteristics of all languages. Chomsky spoke of 'surface' and 'deep structures'. Some sentences contain ambiguities when out of context. A very simple example is, *Old men and women were told to leave the ship.* In this sentence it is not clear whether we are talking about old men and old women or old men and all women.

The ambiguities become more complicated in such sentences as *He was frightened by the policeman's appearance.* This could mean either he was frightened when the policeman appeared or he was frightened by how the policemen looked.

Chomsky developed transformational rules to look at what is

embedded in these sentences. The grammar goes much further than just dealing with these relatively simple sentences.

At one time it was seen as important for language learning. Chomsky himself doubted that it could be used much in language pedagogy. It did and does, however, give insights into features of language which are useful for teachers to consider, such as the examples quoted above.

1.2.5 Functional-systemic grammar

Halliday's functional-systemic grammar aims to make clear the interaction between syntax (form), semantics (meaning) and pragmatics (use). His functional grammar:

1. '. . . is designed to account for how the language is used'
2. looks at the 'fundamental components of meaning';
3. explains 'each element in a language . . . by reference to its function in the total linguistic system'.

(Halliday, 1985).

The Subject–Verb–Object description of language and the categories of the words in the sentence is accepted, but this is at a syntactic level. In order to show the semantic relationship between the components of the sentence, other terms are needed.

There have been other attempts to do this. One approach is the grammar of case. This attempts to show the relationship through the way we identify the different parts. An example is shown in the following analysis of this sentence: *Juliet Solomon wrote 'Holding the Reins'*. In traditional grammar, the sentence would be parsed in this way:

Subject	← Verb	Object
Juliet Solomon	← wrote	'Holding the Reins'.

If we make it passive, *'Holding the Reins' was written by Juliet Solomon*, 'Holding the Reins' becomes the subject.

In neither the active nor passive form is the semantic relationship between Juliet Solomon and 'Holding the Reins' made clear by the categories given to the different components of the sentence. What is shown is only the syntactic organization.

The analysis in the grammar of case is different:

Juliet Solomon	wrote	'Holding the Reins'.
agentive		objective

'Holding the Reins'	was written	by Juliet Solomon.
objective		agentive

The nominal groups are identified in the same way in both the passive and active versions. In this way the semantic role is maintained. For a more detailed account of the grammar of case, see Anderson, J. (1971).

In Halliday's version, <u>Juliet Solomon</u> would be the <u>actor</u> in both of the sentences (Halliday, 1985, pp.30ff.).

The functional–systemic grammar does not ignore the syntactic description of the sentence but looks at the syntactic–semantic relationship. Halliday marks three types of 'subject' – the logical subject, the psychological subject and the grammatical subject. He uses the following examples:

1b
The duke gave my aunt the teapot.
The teapot my aunt was given by the duke.

In the first example, the duke (the actor) represents all three types of subject.

In the second example, the different types of subject are split between the three nominal groups: the teapot is the psychological subject, my aunt is the grammatical subject and the duke is the logical subject.

In identifying these three types of subject, he argues that 'the teapot' is the <u>theme</u> of the sentence, in the sense that it is what the sentence is about. 'My aunt' is the grammatical subject in the sense that it is the subject of the verb. 'The duke' is the logical subject because he is the performer or actor in the action.

ACTIVITY

What types of subject (if any) are the nominal groups in these sentences:

1c
Juliet Solomon wrote 'Holding the Reins'.
'Holding the Reins' was written by Juliet Solomon.

In discussing 'theme', Halliday says:

We may assume that in all languages, the clause has the character of a message: it has some form of organization giving it the status of a communicative event. But there are different ways in which this may be achieved. In English, as in many other languages, the clause is organized as a message by having a special status assigned to one part of it. One element in the clause is enunciated as the theme; this then combines with the remainder so that the two parts together constitute a message. . . . In speaking or writing English we signal that an item has thematic status by putting it first. No other signal is necessary . . . The theme is the element which serves as the point of departure for the message; it is that with which the clause is concerned. . . . The theme is not necessarily a Nominal group . . . It may also be an adverbial group or prepositional phrase. (Halliday 1985: 38–9)

Examples of the different groups that can become the theme is found in two advertisements from 1986. Both advertisements featured the photograph of a prominent person, used to endorse the product.

The first one was advertising Polaroid cameras and featured a photograph of Eddy Shah to endorse the product. At the time the advertisement was released, Eddy Shah was famous in Britain as the person who had introduced computer technology into the production of newspapers, and thus identified as a person who kept in the forefront of modern technological advances. As such, his views on what made up life in the mid-nineteen-eighties would have a large following. Capitalizing on this, the advertiser is attempting to get the reader to identify with Eddy Shah.

The main text of the advertisement is *I'm a believer in instant technology*.

The theme of the copy is not the camera, but the personality. If the reader identifies with the personality (Eddy Shah), he or she will go out and buy the camera. The camera becomes an important accessory for the person who wishes to be seen as being up-to-date and modern.

In this case, however, the text is unmarked and follows the traditional form of S–V–O although, of course, the object is replaced by a complement. The theme in the sentence is the Subject *I*.

In the second advertisement, the same approach has been used. In this case a famous actor, who at the time was the star of the most popular weekly comedy on television in Britain – Yes, Prime Minister – is endorsing a wine: *For me a glass of Veuve Cliquot says summer*.

Here the theme of this first sentence in the text is a prepositional phrase, *For me*. The aim of the advertiser is to get the reader to identify with the actor or his role and then go out and buy the wine. However, the organization of the sentence is not

unmarked as in the one for the Polaroid camera. The prepositional phrase has been moved from its usual place at the end of
the sentence to the beginning. The copywriter has made a choice
between two forms which are both grammatically correct; and
in doing so, has shifted the focus of the sentence from the glass
of Veuve Cliquot to the actor. The shift of focus has been done
by means of the grammar.

ACTIVITY

Some years ago, I asked a number of teachers in various situations around the world to give me their definition of grammar. I
asked both native speaker teachers and non-native speakers.
Overleaf is a selection of ten of the definitions that were sent to
me. Read through the definitions and decide how you would
rate them on a scale of 0–5, where 5 indicates that the definition
is absolutely right and 0 shows that you find the definition
completely inappropriate.

1.3 Approaches to grammar in the classroom

Most people who have considered the definitions overleaf have
found a tension between 'grammar as form' and 'grammar as a
resource for meaning'. This arises because many people are
unsure about where the parameters lie. Where does grammar
end and discourse begin?

In thinking about teaching grammar, there are three areas we
have to consider: grammar as rules, grammar as form and
grammar as resource.

1d

Definitions	5	4	3	2	1	0
1. The structure and framework of the language which governs the use of words.						
2. Grammar is the link between structure and meaning: how meaning is conveyed through structure.						
3. The structure of the language through which we communicate our ideas intelligibly and clearly and acceptably.						
4. The name given to a system of rules by which the words in a language can be organized so that when put together according to those rules, they make sense to the users of that language.						
5. An expression of the relationships between words in sentences.						
6. The conscious/subconscious awareness of the structure of our daily language.						
7. It was traditionally described as a definition of the morphology, phonology and syntax of a language; but all that is now very old hat.						
8. The way people usually say things or write things.						
9. A set of rules laying down how to string words together, and how to change words so that they can be used in certain positions and with certain meanings.						
10. Underlying structure of the language.						

Read sections 1.3.1–1.3.3, then define the term 'grammar' in a way which you think would be most useful for a teacher.

1.3.1 Grammar as rules

For many people, in both the L1 and L2 situation, learning grammar often means learning the rules of grammar. Learners are required to have an intellectual knowledge of grammar. The belief here is that this will provide the basis on which learners can build their knowledge, which will act as the generative base.

1e

USES OF THE DEFINITE ARTICLE
The definite article 'the' is used to mark the phrase it introduces as definite, i.e. as 'referring to something which can be identified uniquely in the contextual or general knowledge shared by the speaker and hearer'.
(Quirk *et al.* 1985: 5.27)

1f

Because 'the' is the commonest specific determiner, you can put 'the' in the front of any common noun:
She dropped <u>the can</u> on <u>the grass</u>.
<u>*The girls*</u> *were not in* <u>*the house*</u>.
In these examples, the use of 'the can' means that a can has already been mentioned; 'the grass' is probably definite because it has already been stated that 'she' is outside, and the presence of grass may also have been stated or is presumed; 'the girls' like 'the can' must have been mentioned before, and 'the house' means the one where the girls were staying at the time.
(Collins COBUILD English Grammar 1990: 1.163)

While the rules I have quoted above might seem rather esoteric, there are simpler rules:

1g

DEFINITE ARTICLE

That is <u>the</u> man I saw at the museum.	→	*to specify*
Men have walked on <u>the</u> moon	→	*for something unique*
He is <u>the</u> funniest teacher.	→	*superlatives*
<u>Spring</u> is our most beautiful season.	→	*no definite article before names, countries, festivals, days, months, seasons, meals, abstract nouns, uncountable and plural countable nouns*

(Bosewitz 1987: 3.5)

Such 'rules' as this can provide the kind of generative base for learners to express ideas and narratives relating to the past. Perhaps 'rules' is too strong a word here, and a term like 'information about the language form' would be more appropriate.

However we choose to refer to it, if the definition of grammar is concerned with the rules which define how forms are composed and used, then we have to see how this can be transferred to actual use.

But are rules important? It is argued by those who also argue that native speakers are always making mistakes in their own grammar, that rules are unimportant, since a child learns to speak its own language and use its own grammar without learning the rules: therefore learning grammar rules is unnecessary.

It is not really as simple as this, however, since the child saying, *'I goed to the park,'* may not have consciously learned or absorbed the rules; but the child has certainly observed what happens when we form the past simple on many occasions, and has unconsciously hypothesized a rule. The child is wrong not because the rule is wrong, but because the child is not yet aware of irregular verbs. Thus it would not be correct to say that children do not acquire rules.

For many people, prescribed rules give a kind of security. We have only to look at the success of such grammars as *A Practical English Grammar* (Thomson and Martinet 1960) or *English Grammar in Use* (Murphy 1985) to see this is so. The weakness of such grammars is that they do not deal with psychological operation of language, so that tense becomes synonymous with time, and explanations become too strong and narrow to reflect actual use.

1.3.2 Grammar as form

Many people see grammar as the form of the structure. This includes the ordering of words, the correct addition of suffixes and prefixes, and the correct use of the article.

Many people can, in fact, make sense of what is said even if there are mistakes in the form used. As far as simple information is concerned, this can be the case. The child saying 'I goed to the park' will have communicated information successfully, albeit grammatically incorrectly.

The danger here is that in identifying grammar with form, the recognition of what is right and what is wrong stays at the level of Subject–Verb agreement, plural markers, possessive markers, tense formation, etc. Rutherford (1980) describes these as low-syntax rules, since concentrating on these, important though they are, often means ignoring the higher level organization of the communication.

There is a dilemma here which many teachers of both L1 and L2 have difficulty in resolving. If the errors in low level-syntax are ignored, then students have no way of measuring how acceptable their use of grammar at that level is. If, on the other hand, all errors of this kind are pointed out, the communicative quality of the work is often lost and students are compelled to focus on very small points at the expense of the larger overall theme. Then we lay ourselves open to the charge that we are not fully concentrating on what the speaker or writer is trying to say.

1.3.3. Grammar as resource

Some way to resolving this dilemma comes about when we consider grammar as a resource.

As we have seen in Halliday, grammar is one of many resources that we have in language which helps us to communicate, and choosing the correct form is as important as choosing the most appropriate lexical item. While form is important here, we are looking at how grammar relates to what we want to say and how we expect our listener or reader to interpret what we are saying and the focus of what we are saying.

So, where are the parameters of grammar? In written language, the organization of the sentence is possibly more important than in the spoken language. In spoken language, the full meaning of the message can be promoted by the manner in which it is said. The pitch and stress used in utterances are also important in conveying meaning or intention, and that is why some grammarians would include phonology within the sphere of grammar.

In the preface of *A Communicative Grammar of English*, Leech and Svartik (1975) discuss the organization of the book, in which they have employed 'a communicative rather than a structural approach'.

In the book, they look at the varieties of English since, as they say, where there is a choice of structures, they are often not equivalent because they belong to different 'styles' or 'varieties', such as formal/informal; spoken/written. They also look at intonation as it 'is clearly important in a communicative treatment stressing spoken English'.

The main part of the book is Grammar in Use. Here there are four sections representing 'a rational progression from the most limited and detailed sphere of meaning to the most inclusive':

Type of meaning or meaning organization	Type of formal unit
A: Concepts	Word, phrase, or clause
B: Information, reality and belief	Sentence
C: Mood, emotion and attitude	Utterance
D: Meanings in connected discourse	Discourse or text

(Leech and Svartvik 1975)

This suggests to me that grammar incorporates all aspects of language; and while most people would probably separate phonology from grammar in the same way that they do vocabulary, all three clearly integrate to give meaning to utterances and to our interpretation of the utterances.

Introducing Grammar

SUMMARY

- It is difficult to give any complete definition of grammar, as people have different views of where the parameters lie.
- The term 'grammar' can itself be used in several different ways, i.e. a book listing grammar rules; an approach to describing language; a school subject.
- There have been several approaches to looking at language, from syntactic descriptions to attempts to show the semantic and pragmatic dimensions of grammar. This is reflected in the different ways grammar has been, and is some cases still is, taught at schools.
- In some cases, grammar lessons have meant learning the rules; in others, practising the form; and in others understanding how grammar helps to convey the meaning and intention of the message.

2   Grammar and communication

2.1 'Good' grammar

In chapter 1, we explored the ways in which grammar has been defined and sought a definition which encompassed the various roles grammar is expected to play by different people: formal rules, syntactic organization, a resource to convey the meaning and intention of what we want to say. In this chapter, we shall examine this last role and look at how grammar helps us to communicate.

ACTIVITY

Look at the five utterances below and decide if there are any circumstances in which they would be considered grammatically acceptable.

2a
— *What you was doing was wrong.*
— *That's him, over there.*
— *I can't do nothing for him.*
— *Put it on table.*
— *It's me who's won the prize.*

Leech *et al.* question what we mean by 'good' and 'bad' grammar:

The terms 'good' and 'bad' do not apply to grammar in the way in which we are using that term in this book. If we view grammar as a set of rules which describe how we use language, the rules themselves are not good or bad, though they may be described adequately or inadequately in a description of how the language works.

Linguists who write grammars are concerned with describing how the language is used rather than prescribing how it should be used. So if it is common for people to use sentences such as *Who did you give this to?*, then the rules of a descriptive grammar must allow for this type of sentence in its rules. Those concerned with prescription, however, might consider this to be an example of 'bad grammar', and might suggest that *To whom did you give this?* would be a better sentence. What is considered better or worse, however, is of no concern to a descriptive linguist in writing a grammar that accounts for the way people actually use language. If people are communicating effectively with language, then they must be following rules, even if those rules are not universally approved. (Leech *et al.* 1982)

For many people, however, form, i.e. Rutherford's low-syntax rules, is the manner in which grammatical structures are manifest. The following scene will not be unfamiliar to many L2 teachers:

STUDENT: *He come next week.*
TEACHER: *'comes'.*
STUDENT: *Yes, he come next week.*

The **usage** of the form is the way people judge other people's command of the language. Within the L1 situation, it can be used to decide how well a person is educated.

In English, this can be shown by Subject–Verb agreement, especially in the past continuous form, where we might hear such examples as: *You was doing that wrong.*

Another common error is the use of the past participle form of *to do* for the simple past, for example, *He done it.*

In German, the correct use of the article *der*, *die* or *das*, i.e. deciding whether a noun is masculine, feminine or neuter, is used in the same way to judge a person's education.

People often feel, however, that grammatical mistakes do not affect our ability to understand what the speaker is trying to say, as these two situations show:

2b

On a New York subway, a Norwegian visitor is apologizing to two New Yorkers, because he knows he has made a lot of grammar mistakes while talking to them

NORWEGIAN: *I'm, sorry. My English grammar is so bad.*
NEW YORKER: *That doesn't matter. We can understand what you're trying to say.*

2c

When I first went to live in Italy, I had trouble in dealing with all the tenses. An Italian friend said, 'Don't worry, Edward. Just use the infinitive. We can work out the tense you want to use'.

In both of these cases, as far as grammar was concerned, what was uppermost in the speakers' minds was the form. In the case of 2b, the visitor had earlier confused the word order. In 2c, I was having difficulty with the way to form the different tenses.

What is clear, however, is that the native-speakers – the New Yorkers in 2b and the Italian in 2c, are concerned with the communication, while grammar seems to play a secondary role.

2.2 Communicative competence

At first, support for the idea that grammar was not important in communication seemed to come from the theory of **communicative competence** put forward by Hymes:

If an adequate theory of language users and language use is to be developed, it seems that judgements must be recognized to be in fact not of two kinds but of four. And if linguistic theory is to be integrated with theory of communication and culture, this fourfold distinction must be stated in a sufficiently generalized way. I would suggest, then, that for language and for other forms of communication (culture), four questions arise:

1. Whether (and to what degree) something is formally possible;
2. Whether (and to what degree) something is feasible in virtue of the means of implementation available;
3. Whether (and to what degree) something is appropriate (adequate, happy, successful) in relation to a context in which it is used and evaluated;
4. Whether (and to what degree) something is in fact done, actually performed, and what its doing entails.

(Hymes 1971: 281)

Consider the following examples, which are correct grammatically:

2d

1. *This is a picture that a girl that a friend of mine knows painted.*
2. *I saw it in a book that a former teacher of mine thought of at one time setting us some exam questions out of.*

(Leech *et al.* 1982)

The sentences fulfil the first criterion, which deals with the strict grammar rules, but they fail in the second, where their length and the number of embedded clauses would make it difficult for the hearer to remember everything and untangle the message.

The third criterion is concerned with appropriacy. While in a very formal situation, such as a court of law, the speaker may ask 'To whom should I give this?', such an utterance would sound wrong in a less formal situation, and may even be considered pompous.

The final criterion is based on whether an utterance would be made by a native speaker and in what circumstances. For example, let us look at the use of *done* instead of *did*. In many dialects in Britain it is possible for people to say, *He done it* or *I done that last week*. As the eastLINC project *Looking at Grammar* states:

Forms in many regional dialects, such as 'done' used as the past tense where Standard English uses 'did', operate according to rules just as Standard English does, but they are different ones. In this case the same form is used for both past tense and past participle, and is analogous to regular forms in Standard English, such as 'I have walked' and 'I walked'. It is not used for other uses of 'did'; no-one says 'Done you write that yesterday?' instead of 'Did you write that yesterday?' (eastLINC 1991)

Another example is the omission of the article in certain Northern dialects in England.

For many people Hymes' model of 'communicative competence' gave a lower profile to grammar, and the emphasis in both L1 and L2 teaching shifted to 'communication', where the aim was to develop tasks and activities which gave students the opportunity to communicate in 'authentic' situations.

If error is occurring in the communication, it is not always possible to decide the point at which grammatical error has or has not led to non-communication. In the case of an L2 speaker, the success of the communication in spite of grammatical error will often depend on the amount of contact the interlocutor has had with L2 speakers, and especially with L2 speakers from a similar language background. Hymes' work was primarily concerned with the communicative competence of L1 speakers.

Canale and Swain (1980) and van Ek (1986) developed models to show communicative competence, with particular reference to L2 speakers. Canale and Swain's model had three major components:
— *Grammatical competence*
— *Sociolinguistic competence*
— *Strategic competence*
  van Ek's model expands these to six:

— Linguistic: produce and interpret meaningful sentences
— Sociolinguistic: awareness of ways in which choice of language forms is determined by setting, relationships, etc.
— Strategic: ways of 'getting our meaning across'
— Discourse: use appropriate strategies in the construction and interpretation of texts
— Socio-cultural: correct and appropriate use (knowledge)
— Social: will and skill to interact with others.

ACTIVITY

Reconsider your comments on the utterances in the activity at the beginning of this chapter.

2.3   The role of grammar

In both Canale and Swain's and van Ek's models, grammatical competence is one of the competences that make up communicative competence. Sociolinguistic competence also has a role to play, where the speaker takes into account the whole context, i.e. the addressee, where the communication is taking place, the occasion when it is taking place, and many other things that fill out the frame of the communication, so that in the majority of cases where two people talking together are using the same language they understand each other.

If grammatical competence is just one of several competences that make up communicative competence, and if many people such as those I've quoted above feel that grammatical errors do not impede communication, why should we consider it important? Close says that:

effective communication depends very largely on a complex set of conventions which both speaker and hearer, writer and reader have to follow and understand. ... If communication is our aim ... then the fact remains that communication can generally be achieved most efficiently by means of a grammatical sentence or by a series of such sentences logically related. (Close 1981: 14)

Nunan (1989), citing support from Littlewood (1981), states that 'grammar is an essential resource in using language communicatively'.

I would like to divide utterances into two parts, Information and Message.

Information

Information is the simple detail of the communication, and it is possible, as I have said above, to convey this with errors, as when a child says *I goed to the park*.

Message

The message conveys much more:

Linguistic meaning conveys a great deal more than reports of events in the real world. It expresses, sometimes in very obvious ways, other times in ways that are hard to ferret out, such things as what is the central part of the message as against the peripheral part, what our attitudes are toward the person we are speaking to, how we feel about the reliability of the message, how we situate ourselves in the events we report, and many other things that make our messages not merely a recital of facts but a complex of facts and comments about facts and situations. (Bolinger 1977: 4)

In summary, the message is made up of:
— the information we wish to convey
— the focus of that information
— our attitude to the information
— our attitude to the receiver

When we communicate, we communicate in messages which contain the complexities shown above. While for many people this may be a very subconscious act, they are not unaware of the force of language. It is not uncommon to hear people say something like 'It's not what s/he said, but the way s/he said it.'

Of course this is all part of communicative competence, and as we have seen there are other competences which are equally important in conveying the message. Grammar is a part of this.

2.4   Grammar as a 'meaning resource'

What is it that makes grammar a meaning resource? How far is the conveyance of a message and the interpretation of the message a subconscious act rather than a conscious act? Obviously, for people whose livelihood depends on their use of language, such as writers, journalists and copywriters, there is a consciousness in how they use the language; but for many people there is an intuitiveness so that they become aware of what is being said although they might not be able to articulate it.

If our only concern is for grammar as form, we find that in some cases there are alternatives which are equally acceptable. It would, therefore, seem to be the case that where there is a choice, the selection must be made on either pragmatic or semantic grounds, otherwise decisions about which form to use would be made on a whim, as if the speaker were saying, 'Today is Monday, so I'll use the active voice. Tuesday is for the passive voice', and in so doing, suggesting that the choice we make makes no difference to the message being conveyed.

As Bolinger says, the choice is there because the choice we make does make a difference to the message we convey.

Let us look at two newspaper reports, in which I have changed the criminal's name. In the first, the reporter has given the reader what appears to be a straightforward account of the arrest of a criminal:

2e

Police searching for a man in connection with ... were last night questioning a man arrested in a west London hotel. Armed anti-terrorist squad detectives surrounded the London Visitors Hotel on Holland Road, Holland Park shortly before	6.00 p.m., after a member of the public told them that the man they were seeking was there. Mr Nat Handsworth, 35, offered no resistance and was taken to Paddington Green police station after his arrest under the Prevention of Terrorism Act.

(*Guardian* 18 April 1986)

2f

... Nat Handsworth – the most wanted man in Britain – was captured last night after a dramatic swoop by armed police. Handsworth, 35, was seized in an early evening raid in West London – nearly thirty hours after	a massive police hunt was launched for him following ... Last night he was being questioned by senior anti-terrorist squad officers at the high security Paddington Green police station in London.

(*Today*, 18 April 1986)

If we examine these texts carefully we can see that the information in each text is exactly the same. However, it is not difficult to see that the focus of the message changes. Whereas in the *Guardian* the focus is much more on the events, in the *Today* newspaper, the reporter is focusing our attention on the criminal. The two reporters are able to achieve the way the message is conveyed simply by the one using the passive voice and the other the active voice. It is in fact the grammar that has caused the shift in focus. And we can see that the selection of the active or passive is important. Of course the form is important, but grammar in this case is much more than form. The selection has been important in conveying the message each writer wished to convey.

Those people who have to persuade us with words use grammar carefully, as the advertisements and the reports on the terrorist show.

As a final example, this is the beginning of a report in a quality newspaper:

2f
Norman Tebbit, a former Secretary of State for Trade and Industry, faces a court-room confrontation ...
(*Independent* 17 May 1990)

It is noteworthy that the reporter chooses the indefinite article when referring to Norman Tebbit's former position in the government. When referring to a former minister's position, it is usual to use the definite article: *Lady Thatcher, the former Prime Minister; Ronald Reagan, the former President of the United States*, etc. The use of the indefinite article here – *Norman Tebbit, a former Secretary of State for Trade and Industry* – makes this a marked statement, and the reader asks why this has happened and makes a special interpretation.

There are two possibilities that come to mind. The most obvious one is that of lowering the status of the former minister, so that he becomes just one of many who have held that post. If we follow on from that, it could be said that the reason for the use of the indefinite article here is that the reporter might be trying to suggest that other Secretaries of State for Trade and Industry are also involved in the affair that is bringing Norman Tebbit to court. The use of the definite article in this case would have suggested that he alone was responsible for what had happened.

ACTIVITY

Look back at the rules for the use of the article quoted in chapter 1.3.1. How would you change them to include the example above?

In all the newspaper texts cited, it is the grammar which has enabled the writer to convey the message intended and the reader to find an interpretation. As such, grammar has been an essential resource in the communications.

Discussing 'models' of language for teaching, Stubbs (1986) says:

it must be a model of how language is interpreted in real-life situations, however simplified and idealized it may be in some respects. It must place centrally the search for meaning which characterizes any use of language. It is a basic finding of linguists that people always attempt to make sense of language which they hear or read. They even do their utmost to make sense out of apparent nonsense, a fact exploited by politicians and advertisers amongst others. (Stubbs 1986: 23)

SUMMARY

- There are variations in the use of the grammar of a language, so that what is not acceptable in one region or dialect will be acceptable in another.
- Using 'good' grammar means communicating well.
- 'Communicative competence' is the ability to use language in the most appropriate way in a specific context and situation.
- Grammar has an important role in helping us to convey our messages.
- Where there are choices, such as whether to use the active or passive voice, which modal to use, or where to use the prepositional phrase, the decision the speaker or writer makes will inform the interpretation of the message by the listener or reader.

3 Grammar and the syllabus

3.1 The role of grammar in language teaching

The first part of the book has considered the importance of grammar in helping us to communicate our ideas and attitudes. In the second part of the book we shall examine what this means in terms of teaching grammar in the language classroom. In this chapter, we shall look at the role of grammar in the language curriculum and the type of syllabus there might be for it.

ACTIVITY

What do you consider to be the main features of a language-learning syllabus?

3.1.1 Grammar in the language curriculum

In talking about the syllabus here, I am referring to an outline of a course, listing and organizing what should be taught.

The importance of grammar within the syllabus, be it in L1 or L2 teaching, has been under discussion for many years. At one time, it was at the core of language teaching in both L1 and L2. In L1, this meant understanding the different parts of speech, such as nouns, verbs, adjectives, adverbs, etc. and being able to understand how sentences were organized. The naming of the parts and the parsing of sentences formed the basis of the grammar class.

In L2, until the Communicative Approach in the 1970s, it was also at the core of learning and teaching. In most cases the grammar was based around the verb patterns discussed in chapter 1. The syllabus, a structural syllabus, was organized around the grammar to be taught.

Teaching 'grammar' became unfashionable not only in the foreign language teaching classroom, but also, in western Europe, in the first language classroom. Although the reasons were different in each case, there was an underlying common belief that learning grammar did not help the learner to communicate well, and in some cases could in fact prove very inhibiting. It was an elitist subject which disadvantaged those pupils from less privileged homes. It made these children very self-conscious and, as a result, they lacked the confidence to take part in discussions, as they felt that they couldn't express their ideas in a manner which would be acceptable, although the ideas themselves were often very pertinent to the discussion. Any emphasis on correct grammar in the classroom rather than the simple articulation of ideas helped to give children with a weaker grasp of language a feeling of inferiority which would affect their attitude to the whole of their school work.

Furthermore, in Britain it was shown that L1 pupils who had been taught grammar were no better or worse in their practical use of the language in spoken discourse or in their writing than those who had not had grammar classes.

In the L2 classroom it was noted that people were able to communicate even if they made mistakes in grammar. Thus there was no need for a focus on grammar, which was seen to be a powerful undermining and demotivating force among L2 learners. Attention, therefore, shifted from thinking of ways of teaching grammar to ways of getting learners to communicate. In the process, grammar was left to swim on its own.

It was as if it had been decided that since all the possible ways of teaching grammar had been investigated and they hadn't worked, grammar should cease to play an important role in language teaching in both L1 and L2 classes.

3.1.2 Attitudes to a grammar syllabus

As I have suggested in chapter 1, there was some confusion about what was meant by 'learning grammar'. When Newmark (1963) says 'The important point is that the study of grammar as such is neither necessary nor sufficient for learning to use a language', he is talking about grammar rules rather than grammar in language use.

Statements such as this (and similar statements were made about L1 classes), coupled with Hymes' definition of communicative competence gave many people the opportunity to question the importance of the role of grammar in a language-learning syllabus, for both the L1 and the L2.

Newmark and Reibel in their 1968 paper were, however, not so much questioning the importance of grammar, but what was being taught as 'grammar'. The dominance at the time of a **behaviourist approach** in L2 teaching, where the focus was on form, was what they were arguing against. They saw the need, as did others, to shift the focus in teaching from the form of language to language in use and to consider grammar within a context and with a content:

We are saying that a chunk of language is most efficiently learned as a unit of form and use. . . .

The pedagogical implication of our position is that we abandon the notion of structural grading and structural ordering of exercise material in favour of situational ordering. . . . the student would learn situational variants rather than structural alternants independent of a contextual base. (Newmark and Reibel 1968)

For many, it was felt that by concentrating on communicative activities, students would naturally acquire the grammar. What is meant by acquire here? A recent definition is:

acquisition (of language) In some theories, language acquisition is opposed to language learning. Acquisition is seen as a more natural process which has parallels with first language development. Acquisition results from meaningful exposure to naturally occurring language and from using it for meaningful communication. Language acquisition results from unconscious and intuitive responses to language. It contrasts with processes of language learning in which explicit knowledge about the forms of a language is presented more regularly for conscious learning. (Carter 1993)

The discussion on learning and acquisition was led by Krashen. Krashen and Terrell (1983) claim that 'If we provide discussion, hence output, over a wide variety of topics while providing communicative goals, the necessary grammatical structures are automatically provided in the input'.

This is almost exactly what was being said about grammar in L1 classes.

In the L2 class, Wilkins (1979) had already made the point that 'the process of being taken systematically through the grammatical system often reduces the motivation of those who need to see some immediate practical return for their (language) learning'.

However, the idea that we should abandon a grammar syllabus was seen as problematic to some. Johnson (1978) saw the problems but felt that there was a way of using a structural syllabus within a communicative approach.

Tongue and Gibbons (1982), however, carried out a small action research task with primary school children in Hong Kong, using a process syllabus based on the needs of the learners. In this case, the syllabus developed out of the perceived needs of the learners at each stage of their learning. The result of this in their 1982 paper suggests that such an approach was successful.

Whatever the thinking about grammar and its importance in communication and in acquiring communicative competence might have been, many L2 teachers, however, have been wary of giving up some kind of system which organizes language. Richards (1985) commented that 'despite the impact communicative approaches have had on methodology in recent years, the bulk of the world's second- and foreign-language learners continue to learn from materials in which the principles of organization and presentation are grammatically based'.

ACTIVITY

Extracts 3a–3d on pages 38–39 are from the contents pages of coursebooks written between 1960 and 1985. What changes do you notice, and can you suggest when each course was written?

Johnston (1985) claimed that 'the language produced by second language learners, and the way in which they learn, is systematic . . . (There is) overwhelming evidence in its favour'.

3.2 Types of syllabus

ACTIVITY

Read sections 3.2.1–4, then decide which types of syllabus 3a–3d on pages 38–39 represent.

3.2.1 The structural syllabus

In spite of the many attempts to develop alternative syllabuses, there is still support for the structural syllabus in L2 teaching. Ellis (1993) says the structural syllabus is useful as a way into the acquisition of grammar. It has a positive role to play in the development of student **consciousness-raising**, which Rutherford has identified as important for internalizing and using language accurately and fluently. It provides the structure on which to build consciousness-raising tasks.

The common factor in the grammar syllabus in both L1 and L2 teaching is that hitherto it has concentrated on syntax. As we have seen, the L2 grammar syllabus was, and in many cases still is, almost mathematical in its structural progression. Difficulties in grammar are equated with the complexities of the form, so that the present perfect is taught at an earlier stage than the possible conditional. However, it might be the case that the concept of the possible conditional is simpler for the learner to grasp than the concept of the present perfect. In his introduction to the chapter on grading tasks, Nunan says:

determining what is grammatically easy or difficult is not quite as straightforward as it might seem. This is partly due to the fact that measurement of grammatical ease and difficulty will vary according to which grammatical system you happen to be following. It is further complicated by the fact that what is easy from the perspective of grammatical analysis is not necessarily that which will be easy to learn, a fact which has been demonstrated by second language acquisition research. For example, Pienemann and Johnston (1987) have been able to demonstrate that while for using the third person singular 's' is fairly simple in terms of grammatical analysis, in terms of speech processing (i.e. the load it places on the learner's short-term memory) it is quite difficult. (Nunan 1989: 5.1)

3a

UNIT 1:
Saturday
Set 1 Identification
Set 2 Invitations
Set 3 Likes and dislikes (1)

UNIT 2:
Peter
Set 2 Description: People
Set 3 Description: Places

UNIT 3:
Peter went away
Set 1 Impatience
Set 2 Not knowing
Set 3 The past (1)
Set 4 Surprise and disbelief

UNIT 4:
Looking for Peter
Set 1 Plans
Set 2 The past (2)

UNIT 5:
Tottenham Motors Limited
Set 1 Ability
Set 2 Polite requests
Set 3 Telephoning
Set 4 Instructions

UNIT 6:
Carlo's kitchen
Set 1 Present interest in past events
Set 2 Experiences

3b

UNIT	MAIN TEACHING POINT	EXPRESSIONS
1 Hello!	I'm/he's/she's/you're a (student) from (England) ● + Q + Neg. + Where . . . from? ● Numbers 1–4 ● Letters A–H	Hello. How are you? I'm very well thanks. And you? I'm fine thanks.
2 Excuse me	We/you/they're (English) ● + Q + Neg. ● Numbers 1–12	Excuse me. Yes? Pardon? Thank you. Yes, please. No, thanks. Please sit down.
3 What is it? What are they?	It/this/that's a (pen) ● + Q + Neg. ● They/these/those are (books) ● + Q + Neg. + What? ● Letters I–Z	
4 What's your name?	What's/are my/your/his/her/our/their job(s)/name(s)? ● Numbers 13–24 ● here/there	Good evening. Over there. Thank you very much. Here's your key.

3c

Unit 1 Present tense of *be*, affirmative sentences, short form replies	Unit 3 Present simple of *speak* and *understand*	Unit 5 Present simple and present continuous tenses contrasted
Unit 2 Present continuous – affirmative negative and interrogative	Unit 4 Present simple of other verbs	Unit 6 Adjectives, position and invariability

3d

	Grammar	Phonology	Functions	Topics and notions
1 to 4	Present tense of *be*; *have got*; *a* and *an*; noun plurals; subject personal pronouns; possessives; possessive *'s* and *s'*; predicative use of adjectives; questions (question word and yes/no); *be* with ages; prepositions of place; *this*; *any* in questions.	Word and sentence stress; rhythm; linking; intonation; consonant clusters; /θ/ and /ð/; /ɪ/; /ə/; pronunciation of *'s*; weak form of *from*.	Greet; introduce; begin conversations with strangers; participate in longer conversations; say goodbye; ask for and give information; identify themselves and others; describe people; ask for repetition; enquire about health; apologise; express regret; distinguish levels of formality; spell and count.	People's names; age; marital status; national origin; addresses; jobs; health; families; physical appearance; relationships; numbers and letters; approximation; place.
5 to 8	Simple present tense; *there is** *are*; imperatives; *was* and *were* (introduction); countable and uncountable; *some*/*any*, *much*/*many* and other quantifiers; *the*; omission of article in generalizations; object personal pronouns; attributive use of adjectives; frequency adjectives; adverbs of degree; prepositions of time, place and distance; omission of article in *at home* etc.; *-ing* for activities; *be* with prices.	Word and sentence stress; rhythm; linking; intonation, including polite intonation; weak forms; /ɪ/; /θ/ in ordinals; pronunciations of *the*.	Ask for and give information, directions, personal data, and opinions; describe places; indicate position; express likes and dislikes; tell the time; complain; participate in longer conversations; express politeness.	Addresses; phone numbers; furniture; houses and flats; work; leisure occupations and interests; food and drink; prices; likes and dislikes; preferences; things in common and differences; days of the week; ordinal numbers; existence; time; place; relative position; generalization; countability; quantification; degree; frequency; routines.

Work has been done researching the stages in which learners acquire the grammar of the target language. Ravem (1974) claimed learners could use *do*-support in *Yes/No* questions before they could use it in *Wh-* questions, i.e. they could formulate correctly the question *Does he come?* but they would still say *What he did?*

There have been many studies made regarding the order in which morphemes are acquired. Cook (1991) records that made by Dulay and Burt:

3e

L2 LEARNING OF GRAMMATICAL MORPHEMES

L2 learners have a common order of difficulty for grammatical morphemes, first discovered by Dulay and Burt

1. plural -s   'Books'
2. progressive -ing   'John going'
3. copula be   'John is here'
4. auxiliary be   'John is going'
5. articles   'The books'
6. irregular past tense 'John went'
7. third person -s   'John likes books'
8. possessive 's   'John's books'

Richards (1984) pointed out that these studies are of little significance unless they are related to a theory of the development of language proficiency, while Cook notes that this has had little influence on the organization of the grammatical syllabus in recent course books. He makes a comment similar to Richards':

There has been controversy about these sequences of morphemes. The overall problem is that, while this research discovered a 'natural order' of difficulty, it did not find an explanation for this order. Without an

explanation it can only have a limited relevance to teaching. ...
researchers have come to realise that it is not necessarily true that
things that are easy to use are learnt first and vice versa, even if in
many cases this is true. An order of acquisition cannot be based solely
on an order of difficulty. (Cook 1991)

In L2, we also have to consider if there is a difference between
child and adult learners. There is some evidence to suggest that
the age of the learner has to be taken into consideration. Bruton
(1984), working with a mixed group of young and older students
in Spain, found that while the older students felt the need for a
more organized approach, the younger ones worked well with
something unstructured. Perhaps this was what was working in
the investigation carried out by Tongue and Gibbons (see 3.1.2).

I am not saying that age is a factor in determining ability to
acquire a second or foreign language and, indeed, Singleton
(1981) said there was scant evidence for this. It means, however,
that the approach we need to take will be different for children
from that for adults.

Be that as it may, what are our goals for both L1 and L2
learners? Carter summarizes the Cox committee recommendations for the National Curriculum in England and Wales in this
way:

For grammar to be relevant to English teaching, it must
— relate to language in use
— be described with reference to actual purposes and real contexts
  rather than as a part of a set of decontextualized exercises
— focus on functions as well as on forms
— have educational relevance: that is, be of demonstrable use in, for
  example, differentiating spoken from written English
— be related to the study and use of texts in educational contexts – that
  is, be seen as a central meaning-making component in the organization of different kinds of text
— be seen as a part of a wider syllabus of language study
(Carter 1991: 20)

THE GRAMMAR PIE

3f

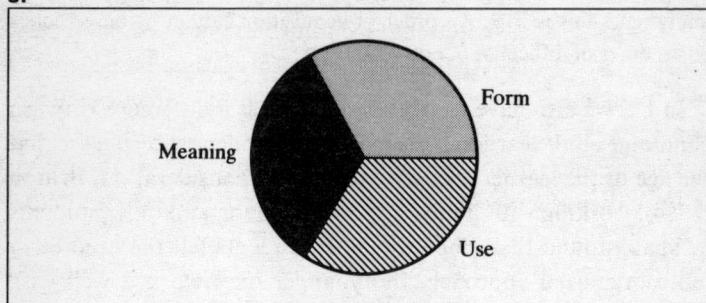

3g

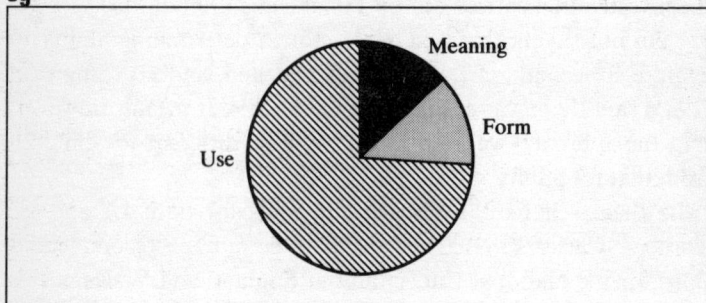

3h

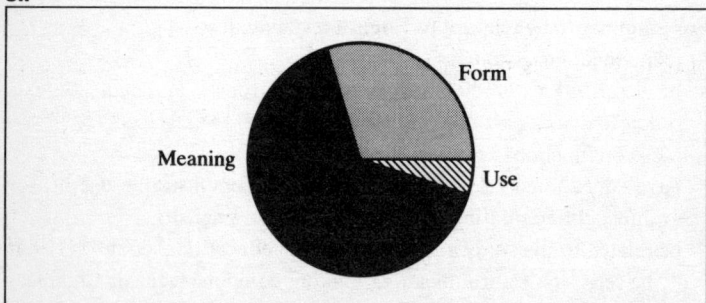

(Based on Larsen–Freeman 1991)

These suggest there is a similarity of aims in L1 and L2 syllabuses. Where differences occur is at the starting point. L2 learners have to start from the base where they have a knowledge of a language and, therefore, albeit unconsciously or intuitively, some knowledge about language, but this is not based on the target language. L1 learners actually have the target language, though they will not be in full control of it.

The syllabus must guide the learner in moving from knowledge of form to grammatical competence within the total communicative competence.

In talking about L2 learners, Larsen-Freeman (1991) suggests a grammar pie to help resolve this problem (see 3f–3h). The portions of the pie are not fixed, and the teacher can cut the portions to whichever size is appropriate for the lesson and for the students.

This will depend on several things, such as what stage the learners are in their language learning, what their first language is and, therefore, what kind of problem is presented by the new structure; how far this is the first appearance of the structure or whether it is being recycled; the age and interests of the learners.

Let us take as an example the passive. At the first introduction, learners must clearly learn to manipulate the form. But for most learners this is not something on which they need to spend a lot of time. Exercises such as this one are useful:

3i

Jerry Keen came home soon after a crime had taken place in his house. He is telling the police what he saw.
  Use the words under each picture to make sentences.

1. a window/break
    (= **A window had been broken, but I've no idea who broke it.**)

2. the radio/
    turn on

3. the dog/tie up

(Adamson and Cobb 1987: p.3)

There are, however, more important aspects of the passive in use that learners need to know. (The grammar task book from which the above task was taken gives other exercise types showing this.) My experience has been that students have little idea when or where to use the passive, scattering it around essays quite randomly, seemingly to show that they know how to form the passive.

As with all grammar structures, we can immediately identify two stages for teaching: the form and the use. Thus, for the first stage our grammar pie would be divided as in pie 3f on p.42. At the second stage, it would be divided as pie 3g.

These stages require different input and different tasks. The syllabus, however, is still a structural one. Where, in the past, teachers became disillusioned with it was that there was essentially a focus on form. If there is a proper recycling process, the structural syllabus will focus on the higher levels of meaning and use.

3.2.2   The functional–notional syllabus

As the focus on form in the structural syllabus was found to be unsatisfactory, an alternative system started to emerge that shifted the focus from the form of grammatical structures to their functional use.

Wilkins (1972) discussed the idea of a functional–notional syllabus. Such a syllabus was intended to bring together the formal organization of grammar with the functional use of language. The functional part of the syllabus would look at what people do with language: apologize, persuade, request, etc. The notional part was concerned with grammar. The approach to grammar, however, was not to look at discrete structures, but to see how the grammar was used in larger units. Wilkins divides his categories of notions into two sections. The first, which he calls semantico–grammatical categories, 'contribute to the definition of the grammatical content of learning'. These are concepts such as time, quantity, space, case and **deixis** and a category he calls matter.

The second section he describes as 'categories of communication'. These are modality, moral evaluation and discipline, suasion, argument, rational enquiry, personal emotions, emotional relations and interpersonal relations. For a fuller discussion of these, you should read Wilkins (1979) original papers or van Ek's *The Threshold Level* (1977).

The Council of Europe drew up a list of functions and notions which learners at what they called the 'threshold' level should be able to perform in the L2. The aim was to apply this across all languages, so that there could be common criteria against which a learner's performance could be judged.

The charm of functions is that they are obviously a means for looking at 'language in use', and the focus is on language in use rather than simply on form. The focus was moving from use to usage, in Widdowson's 1978 terms. This was 'language in context', as Newmark and Reibel (1968) suggested.

The functions of language were relatively easy to identify and explain. Students could be shown that a question is not always asked by using the interrogative form, but can be made through a statement with a raised intonation pattern: *You were in London yesterday?*

The role of meaning was also highlighted: *It's very cold in here.* This can be a simple truth statement about the temperature in the room; but it could also be a way of suggesting a window should be closed, or a request for the heating to be put on.

This focus on what you do with language, rather than on how language is organized was at the basis of a lot of the graded objectives models in foreign language teaching in British schools, where the syllabus was organized around what the students would be able to do in the foreign language at the end of defined periods, without an emphasis on correct use of grammar.

Course books in the late 1960s and 1970s started to claim that they were functional. However, on closer examination, many of them also followed a structure-based syllabus. With a purely functional syllabus, problems arise because utterances are often multi-functional. Attempts, for pedagogical purposes, to illustrate a function through a single sentence or statement are very close to reverting to the idea of the superiority of form over meaning and content. Only, this time, it is the form of the function rather than the grammatical form.

Furthermore, functions themselves are not generative in the way structures can be. Having learned that *Couldn't we go the cinema this evening?* carries the function of suasion does not help us either to consider other forms with the same function or lead us on to other functions. Learning how to persuade does not lead us towards the function of apology. Brumfit made the point that:

> The syllabus itself will be specified grammatically, because syntax is the only generative system so far described for language, and – since time is at a premium – a generative system will be more economical as a way of organizing language work for student learning than a non-generative taxonomy of items (such as a list of functions is bound to be), or a random selection of items, unsystematically collected. (Brumfit 1981)

Learning the forms of grammar is generative. Learners can build their own rules. They observe what is happening in the language and form hypotheses about the language which they can test. If the hypothesis is right, they have made progress and can now express a large number of statements and ideas in the context of the structure they have been considering.

Wilkins' idea had been that the notional syllabus should interface the functional syllabus. In this way, learners would be able to see the relationship between form, meaning and use. However, even with Wilkins' descriptions, notions were difficult to define and what happened was that the syllabus that developed was more a structural–functional one.

The notional syllabus has not been abandoned. There is still a lot of interest as teachers try to find ways to avoid the situation described by Tarone and Yule:

> Grammar textbooks available to learners in 1981 might lead them (learners) to expect that tense choice is made solely in relation to time – not in relation to the level of generality or the truth value of the content being reported. (Tarone and Yule 1989: 49)

3.2.3 Grammar in the British National Curriculum

In L1 teaching, however, there is an attraction towards a functional–notional type of syllabus. The recommendations of the Cox Committee (see 3.2.1, p. 41) seem to incorporate many of those ideas.

While the functional–notional syllabus may not be satisfactory in itself, it is possible that it could be incorporated with other parallel syllabuses, such as those based on situations or topics. The National Curriculum Council's non-statutory guidance for Modern Foreign Language teaching organizes a syllabus in this way (see opposite).

The interesting thing about this scheme is that, while the first two columns are a mixture of functions and situations, the third column is, until level 10, a structural syllabus. It is also interesting to note how that is organized. It starts with a pre-sentence period, and it is only at the third stage that the learner starts to complete sentences.

The table opposite covers a long period in the language classroom and is based on one particular topic. It does, however, offer insights into where grammar can be placed within a more contextualized and communicative programme.

A problem could be that grammatical structures are forced into situations/topics in an inauthentic way.

3.2.4 The lexical syllabus

A second alternative to the structural syllabus is Willis' lexical syllabus. In setting out his proposals for this, he says:

The process of syllabus design involves itemizing language to identify what is to be learned. Communicative methodology involves exposure

Level	Tasks	Topic content	Language content
1	Naming	Dates, names, saints	Nouns; dates; noun-phrases
2	Describing	Presents for a special occasion	Nouns; adjectives
3	Relating	A family meal for an occasion	Present tense of verbs, first person singular/plural
4	Sharing experiences	Survey of how other people celebrate birthdays	Second and third persons, plus negatives of verbs
5	Comparing	A religious event in other countries or communities	Plurals; making comparisons; adverbs
6	Planning	Invitations	Future tense; question forms; 'modal' verbs
7	Reporting	A recent school event (e.g. gala; school musical)	Past tense
8	Imagining	A 'round the world' tour won in a prize competition	Conditional tense
9	Reading and comparing	Different reports of a national feast day or holiday	Complex sentences
10	Debating	Expressing opinions, with reasons, on marriage	Adapting language for different audiences

(National Curriculum Council 1992: table 14)

to natural language use to enable learners to apply their innate faculties to recreate language systems. There is an obvious contradiction between the two. An approach which itemizes language seems to imply that items can be learned discreetly, and that the language can be built up from an accretion of these items. Communicative methodology is holistic in that it relies on the ability of learners to abstract from the language to which they are exposed, in order to recreate a picture of the target language.

The lexical syllabus attempts to reconcile these contradictions. (Willis 1990: viii)

The Lexical syllabus does not ignore grammar, but looks at it from a different standpoint. The complaint that Willis makes is that in the structural syllabus the focus is principally on the verb and often on form. By shifting the focus to the lexical item, the syllabus becomes one that is much more semantically oriented. The application of this syllabus is to be found in the Collins COBUILD English Course (Willis and Willis 1989).

As an example he looks at the use of *would*, commonly taught as a part of the second conditional. He argues that although 'many ELT grammars and coursebooks talk about the three conditionals . . . there are actually a very large number of possible conditional patterns'. Furthermore, all modals are common in conditional sentences. Thus, in his argument what is required is that learners should know what *if* means and what all the modals mean, and then they will be able to generate conditional sentences. What they have to know about *would* is not how it is used in the second conditional, but that its main meaning is of hypothesis.

The advantage that the structural syllabus has at the moment is that it comes ready-made. The organization of the functional–notional syllabus is still not clear. Willis himself admits that with the lexical syllabus used in the COBUILD course, they had to decide the ordering of the components as they developed the course.

This may be no bad thing, in that one of the dangers facing the structural syllabus is that it has become fossilized and doesn't react to learners' needs.

Whatever approach we take to the syllabus, the professed aim of all those mentioned is to move learners from a knowledge of form towards an ability to understand how they can express what they want to say. In this we have to be careful that we do not impose meaning on to form. Halliday makes the point:

... once the forms had been established, the question was then posed: 'what do these forms mean?' A language is interpreted as a system of meanings, accompanied by forms through which the meanings can be realized. The question is rather: 'how can these meanings be expressed?' This puts the forms of the language in a different perspective: as means to an end, rather than as an end in themselves. (Halliday 1985: xiv)

To support what Willis has said, an example of this at its worst can be found in the way the English conditional is described. Many grammar books in the past, and some still do, talk about the three conditionals:

3j
1. *If* + *simple present, will* + *main verb.*
2. *If* + *simple past, would* + *main verb.*
3. *If* + *past perfect, would have* + *main verb.*

To each of these variations, a meaning is given:

3k
1. *very probable, almost certain*
2. *possible, but unlikely*
3. *impossible*

Chalker prefers to look at ways of expressing the conditional in terms of:

Open (or real) condition – open because the events described are a real possibility, already or in the future.
Hypothetical (or 'rejected') condition – where the condition is 'rejected' as unreal now – although in some cases they could happen later.
(Chalker 1984)

She then goes on to give examples showing different ways in which the conditional can be expressed. Learners can get the impression that the conditional form represented by the *If*-clause is how to express a condition, but very often that is not the case.

Conditionals can be realized by other forms, for example, *Don't undercharge, or you could quickly go out of business.* What is disingenuous in the way the conditional forms have hitherto been taught is that a meaning has been given to each form which has more to do with making the form fit into the teaching pattern than in helping learners to find out how to express the concepts of condition.

The coursebook syllabuses, 3a–3d on pp. 38–39, were:

3a: Abbs *et al.* 1975. *Strategies* – functional.
3b: Hartley and Viney, 1978. *Streamline English – Departures* – structural/functional.
3c Wakeman, 1967. *English Fast* – structural.
3d Swan and Walter, 1990. *The New Cambridge Course* – structural/functional/communicative.

3.3 Developing the syllabus

If we take into account all of the things involved in language and communication, a possible model of the syllabus should include all these areas (see opposite).

The top line involves features concerned directly with language and the lower line things involved within the contexts of learning and of language application.

While this chapter is concerned only with the 'grammar' part of the syllabus, it is important to see it in relation to all the other parts, since what is done in one will affect what happens in the other. For example, how grammar is taught will demonstrate 'learning strategies' to learners which must be appropriate

CONTENT AREAS IN A COMMUNICATIVE SYLLABUS

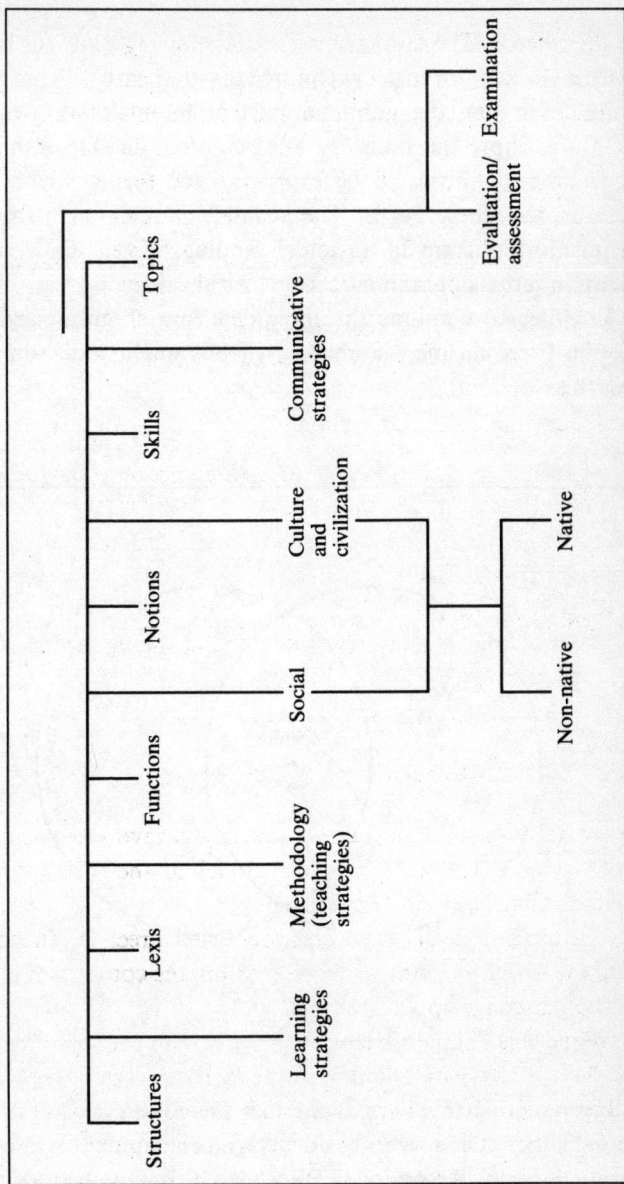

to their needs. The tasks chosen must be appropriate for helping learners to acquire and/or reinforce the grammar.

In developing the grammar part of the syllabus, we might start with <u>how</u> the language is structured, i.e. the form; then consider <u>what</u> needs to be expressed and seeing which forms best express these needs. The syllabus should move from the acquisition of form to an understanding of and ability to use forms in terms of grammatical-rhetorical values.

In order to combine the three elements of grammar in the Larsen-Freeman pie, the model syllabus might look something like this:

3m

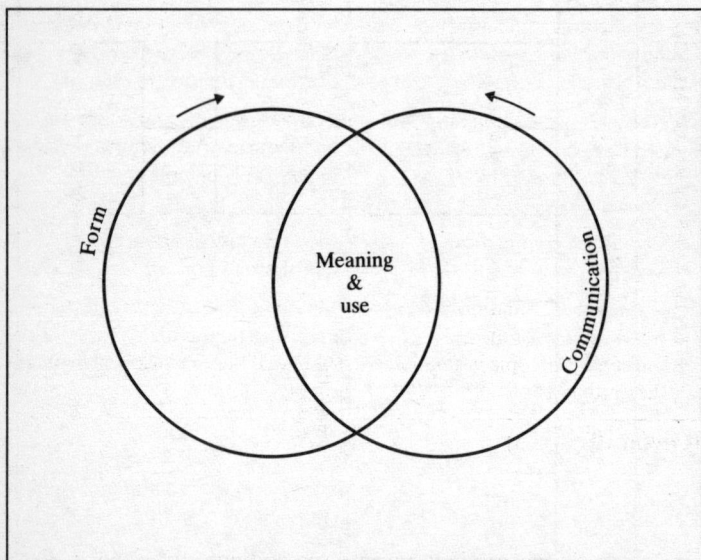

In presenting this I am aware that there is a concentration on form. James Asher, who has developed the approach known as Total Physical Response (TPR), feels this is unnecessary. He said in a BBC film in 1981 that children at an early age should be given opportunities to use the language. At a later age, there could be opportunities to 'fine-tune' their use of grammar.

Givón seems to support this. He identifies the pragmatic mode and the syntactic mode of language development.

Pragmatic Mode	Syntactic Mode
a. Topic–comment structure	Subject–predicate structure
b. Loose conjunction	Tight subordination
c. Slow rate of delivery (under several intonation contours)	Fast rate of delivery (under a single intonational contour)
d. Word-order is governed mostly by one pragmatic principle; old information goes first, new information follows	Word-order is used to signal semantic case-functions (though it may also be used to indicate pragmatic–topicality relations)
e. Roughly one-to-one ratio of verbs-to-nouns in discourse, with the verbs being semantically simple	A larger ratio of nouns-over-verbs in discourse, with the verbs being semantically complex
f. No use of grammatical morphology	Elaborate use of grammatical morphology
g. Prominent intonation–stress marks the focus of new information; topic intonation is less prominent	Very much the same, but perhaps not exhibiting as high a functional load, and at least in some languages totally absent

(Givón 1979: 223)

The pragmatic mode is common in Pidgins and Creoles, Child versus adult language and informal as opposed to formal language.

In looking at reasons for this in child language (and also in Pidgins), he finds three common causes:

— Communicative stress, where there is a need to communicate but no shared mode of communication;
— Lack of common pragmatic background, where there is a lack of background knowledge and shared culture. There is no presuppositional background.
— Immediately obvious context, where the tasks and topics concern the here-and-now.

A subsequent suggestion in **SLA** has been that the pragmatic mode of communication is the natural initial stage in language acquisition.

The Givón model suggesting how learners acquire their L1, or even L2, should not, however, be seen as a reason for ignoring grammar at the initial stage of learning. On the contrary, it shows grammar should be taught in terms of a refining tool, so that learners become aware of its importance in conveying precisely what they want to mean. Halliday (1985) shows that meaning is an interpretation of form and thus the two have a symbiotic relationship.

I do not think that the Givón model suggests that there should be a concentration on fluency as opposed to accuracy. It is important that there should be a focus on grammar from the beginning. What teachers have to be aware of is what in L2 is known as **interlanguage** (Corder 1967 and Selinker 1972), that is, the stage where learners have become aware of some part of the system, but have not yet internalized it well enough to be able to use it accurately.

What it also suggests is that 'grammar as rules' might also have a part to play in the later stages of the syllabus as we fine-tune the learner's control of the language.

Because of the frustration learners have had with grammar, teachers have tried to find a way round the problem instead of facing it and putting grammar near the centre of the syllabus.

Rea-Dickins and Woods talk about their work at the Freie

Universitat (Berlin), at the University of Dar-es-Salaam and at Lancaster University. They found there was a commonality of problems faced by all students, whatever their background:

The problems faced by some of our students arose from their need to communicate at a rather sophisticated level in English when their linguistic competence was at a very low level. This is not to say that they were unable to communicate; most of them were able to do so, albeit in a very confused and/or simple form. They managed to express most of their ideas in English, but in a way that did not do themselves justice as intelligent, educated individuals. Often at the heart of the matter were their use of grammar and their inability to manipulate structure and form in such a way as to convey messages with their full force.

It became apparent to us that the development of communication skills should include not only language and study-skills areas but also the improvement of grammatical competence. (Rea Dickins and Woods 1988)

What is lacking is a clear identification of goals. We rarely look beyond grammar at a sentence level, as is shown by a lot of error correction where the teacher focuses on form, which in many ways is what the student expects. The syllabus proposed by Yalden attempts to move beyond form to grammar in use in communication.

The problem for the 'grammar' syllabus is the term 'communication', which can involve things other than just the use of language, such as gestures and other body language. It is now accepted that L1 learners need to have an understanding of what grammar is, and this is likely to be the case for L2 learners. Thus, for the 'grammar' syllabus it would perhaps be better to replace the term 'communication' with 'language awareness', i.e. how language is used to convey effectively the message, as referred to by Bolinger (1977). See 2.3 p. 27.

In order to achieve this language awareness, there is the need for a series of goals for grammatical achievement to be set out, which move from form to an awareness on the part of the learners of how best to express what they want to convey. This in turn will mean a methodology which provides students in

3n

THE PROPORTIONAL SYLLABUS

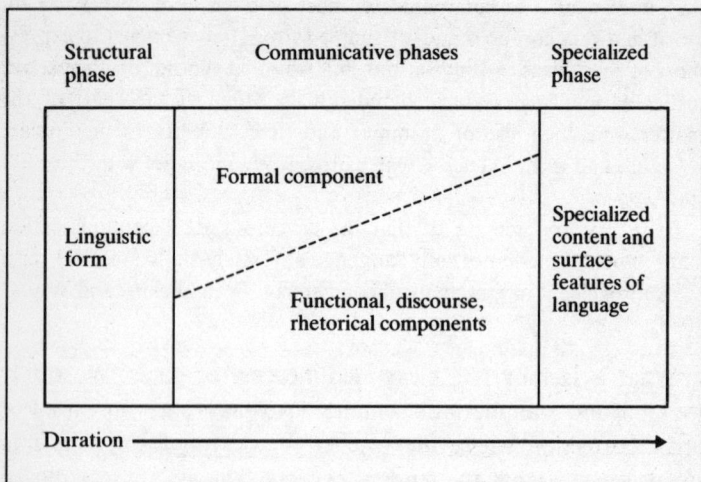

Structural phase	Communicative phases	Specialized phase
Linguistic form	Formal component Functional, discourse, rhetorical components	Specialized content and surface features of language

Duration ⟶

(Yalden 1983: 124)

both the L1 and L2 classroom with the opportunity to do more than focus on a single grammatical structure, but rather will help them to use language to focus on what they really want to say or write about.

We have to remember throughout all this that grammar is just one aspect of communication, albeit an important one. If this is the case, then the grammar syllabus must be one aspect of a larger syllabus looking at other areas which involve both the methodology and the context within which the language is taught.

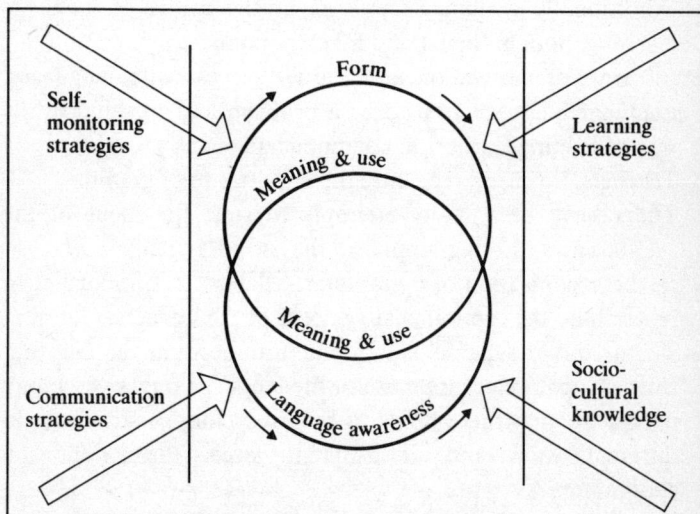

This is intended to represent a cyclical model, where the teacher and learner are continually looking at structures and recycling them to put together a whole view of language.

What we can be sure of is that grammar should have a lead role in the organization of a language teaching/learning programme. In spite of the difficulties learners have had with grammar, many of them expect it to be there and see it as central to their knowledge of the language. Sexton and Williams (1984) cited an informal survey made by members of the Bundearbeitsgemeinschaft Englisch an Gesamtschulen in Germany which showed that many people who had learned languages at school were aware of the fact that they couldn't speak them, had been bored by the insistence on grammar, but thought that everybody should learn grammar. This is the case in both the L1 and the L2 classroom.

SUMMARY

- Traditionally grammar has been at the centre of language teaching, both in the L1 and L2 classrooms.
- In terms of motivation and learner success with languages, grammar has been seen to be a problem and to stand in the way of helping learners to communicate fluently.
- Teachers, however, recognize the importance of grammar.
- There have been many attempts to shift the focus of the syllabus away from grammar to the use of language.
- In the organization of a grammar syllabus, it is important to understand the communicative needs of the learners.
- The grammar syllabus has to take into account the fact that learners acquire accurate use of the language only over a long period, so that there needs to be a recycling of structures in different ways and at different levels throughout the programme.

4   Grammar and methodology

4.1   Different methodologies

For some teachers, syllabus and methodology complement each
other so closely that it is difficult to separate the one from the
other. The goal of the syllabus can determine the methodology
for learning. The history of language teaching is strewn with the
bodies of methodologies abandoned and then resurrected. This
chapter considers what methodology is appropriate for helping
students to understand and use grammar effectively to communicate their messages.

Until the Communicative Approach took hold in the 1970s,
grammar was at the core of L2 learning/teaching. In most cases
the grammar syllabus was based around the verb patterns discussed in chapter 1. Views of grammar were not the same,
however, in the different methodologies. A very good survey of
the different methodologies and approaches is in Richards and
Rodgers (1986), so I will refer you to that and make only brief
comments here on the major ones.

ACTIVITY

No method or approach should be considered to be completely
wrong. As you read through the different methods below, make
a list of the strengths and weaknesses in each one.

4.1.1 The grammar-translation method

The teaching of grammar in the first half of the century was dominated by the grammar-translation method. The emphasis in this method is on the organization of language at sentence level in terms of parts of speech, such as subject, verb, object, and also the types of word, such as noun, verb, adjective, adverb. Its goals were based on the idea that the purpose of learning a foreign language was to read its literature and to benefit from the mental discipline and intellectual development in learning a foreign language. Translation was seen as a way of studying and analysing the rules of the language. Its focus was on rules; and the grammar class came to be seen as the class teaching the rules of grammar.

4.1.2 The Direct Method

The Direct Method, sometimes known as the Natural Method, was based on the belief that a language could best be taught by its active use in the classroom. There was no translation; and the focus on explaining and analysing the rules of grammar was replaced by actual use in the classroom. In this way, learners would be able to induce the rules of grammar. The emphasis was on spoken language, and in the early stages the teacher replaced the text book. Its approach to grammar, however, was not at all systematic.

4.1.3 The oral approach

The oral approach may seem to be very similar to the Direct method in that the emphasis was on the spoken language, but it was based on a much more systematic view of language. In the work of applied linguistics in the early part of the century, such as Palmer and Hornby, there had been attempts to analyse English and classify its major grammatical structures into sentence patterns. In the approach these patterns became the substitution tables that were used to help learners, of which 4a is an example.

4a

He She They We	did it sold it worked late made lunch	because	I wanted he told he ordered she liked	him her them us	to.

The structures were often situationalized to provide a context to help the learners, but even so the exercises stood alone and their only relevance was that they presented a pattern for students to practise. The organization for a lesson would be:

presentation → practice → consolidation → testing → free stage

4.1.4 The audio-lingual method

The audio-lingual method was based on a behaviourist approach to learning. The language was broken down into grammatical structures, which learners practised by means of drills which were concerned with giving students practice is forming correct sentences. An example of such a drill is:

4b

David runs ten miles every day.

.... walks ....

Sheila ....

.... to work ....

............to school...............

Robert..............................

.... cycles......................

.......................once a week.

Initially, the problem here was that all the grammar work was done out of context. Attempts were made to overcome this by putting the practice into situations.

At the time small books and papers were published which listed situations that could be used with the appropriate grammatical structure. For example, the student is shown the picture of a house in need of repair which someone has just bought. The student is encouraged to produce as many sentences as possible using the form:

4c

They had to have the door repaired.

.........................the roof..........

.........................the garden......

However, the problem that arose here was that grammatical structures don't fit conveniently into any one situation and the whole exercise became very artificial. What we had very often were little more than rather sophisticated forms of drills, which many learners still found boring.

4.1.5 The communicative approach

As we have seen, to make language learning relevant and interesting, at the outset of the communicative approach there was a determined movement away from grammar as the centre of a language-learning course. The aim was that the use of language should be the dominant feature.

However, it became evident that where grammar was given little importance, learners soon became very fluent but often very inaccurate, as shown in Rea-Dickins and Woods (1988). We had, in fact, thrown out the baby with the bathwater; and we needed to look at much of what we had done before to see if, by adding some extra dimension, we could develop grammar tasks that were communicative to suit the approach. Rather than teaching communicative grammar, which to my mind gives a wrong emphasis, we had to think about how to teach grammar for communication.

4.2 Teaching grammar for communication

To teach grammar for communication successfully, we have to look at three areas: learner variables, teacher roles and interactive methodology.

4.2.1 Learner variables

In fact, teachers have never really abandoned grammar, but the problem has been how to teach it and what role the learner plays in finding out about grammar rather than being told about it.

ACTIVITY

Consider the different situations you could find in classrooms depending on who the learners are and their needs.

In a paper in 1985, Celce-Murcia listed several variables that need to be taken into account in language learning.

4d

LEARNER VARIABLES			
Age	children	adolescents	adults
Proficiency level	beginning	intermediate	advanced
Educational	preliterate; no formal education	semi-literate; some formal education	literate; well educated

(Celce-Murcia 1985)

4e

INSTRUCTIONAL VARIABLES			
Skill	listening, reading	speaking	writing
Register	informal	consultative	formal
Need/Use	survival communication	vocational	professional

(Celce-Murcia 1985)

What these variables might indicate, as Celce-Murcia goes on to suggest, is that a different approach and methodology needs to be applied depending on where the learners fit into the tables above and what their aims are.

We also have to remember that we are talking about a communicative approach and not a specific methodology. Although we are trying to find ways of making grammar learning interactive, there is no reason why task types and activities associated with older methodologies need not be given an extra dimension to make them interactive, so that we move away from Baudelaire's *l'aride grammaire*. By this, I do not mean that we simply take exercises from course books and have them done in pairs or groups instead of by individuals. What is needed is an extra dimension added to these exercises, such as I will discuss in chapter 5.

The essential thing about communicative activities is that they should promote interaction among the learners and with the teacher. What we are looking at is essentially not the activity itself, but the relationship that exists between the interactors in the activity.

The overuse of the term 'communicative' has led us to ignore, overlook or even reject ways of learning that learners often feel comfortable and happy with. Fortune (1992) reported on some small scale research among students at the Thames Valley University in London. The students were given a battery of different task types and asked to decide which they preferred. He admits that on this small scale the results can hardly be called conclusive, but it gives us some insights into how students prefer to learn. Some of the conclusions are of interest:

4f

— *seeing a rule is for many an important prop;*
— *these students would appear to concur with Eisenstein (1987) who, in a discussion on classroom grammar teaching, argues that 'both deductive and inductive presentation can be useful depending on the cognitive style of the learner and the structure to be presented'. She puts the case for a compromise methodological position where learners attempt to discover a rule from selected language data, then compare it with pedagogic grammar, and finally do more practice of the structure(s) concerned;*

— *many difficulties could be overcome with appropriate classroom learner training beforehand;*
— *The value of non-linguistic information as a basis for language work has long been recognized, but if we wish it to motivate, the subject matter must be less mundane.*

One student complained about having to repeat a structure so often that she started thinking about something else. Finally she commented: 'Anyway, I'm not interested in car hire charges'.

4.2.2 Teacher roles

It seems to me that we have often failed in getting at the true nature of the communicative task. Tasks are not 'communicative' *per se*; it is the classroom situation that makes them communicative.

When it comes to grammar practice tasks, we would be unwise to reject everything that has gone before, such as drills or substitution tables. What we need to do is to look at these afresh in the light of what we feel about the roles in the classroom of the teacher and the learners.

ACTIVITY

Look again at the methods described at the beginning of this chapter and consider what roles teachers and learners would have in each case. How would these roles change in a 'communicative' class?

In the classroom few of us would accept the authoritarian teacher who stands in the front and continues with the lesson irrespective of what the learners have achieved, but is only concerned with the syllabus and the place that has been reached on that.

However, it is also true that many learners find the teacher in the role of facilitator at its most extreme equally disturbing. A middle way is needed, and to find this we need to look at the roles of the teacher and the learners.

In talking about roles, I do not want to take the approach that teachers and learners play many different roles in the course of their work and in the course of a class; but I want to look at three macro-roles that have been considered appropriate for teachers.

In the methods discussed in 4.1.1–4, the teacher dominated the class and played a very authoritarian role. If we take this to its extreme, we will see that the teacher has a controlling role and is the informant. It is the teacher who organizes the classroom, usually in a very formal setting, and the course for which s/he prescribes the objectives. S/He manages the time, i.e. determines how much time may be allowed for each thing that is to be taught. Such teachers insist on accuracy, which inhibits students from taking any chances or risks. The interaction in such a class is only teacher to student, where the teacher has two thirds of the time available. Such a class is frequently organized around exam needs, which help to create an atmosphere of security. While it is always difficult to know what learners have learned, it will be clear to all the learners what they have been taught. This role is best summed up in the diagram in 4g on page 70.

At the other extreme, there is the role of the teacher as facilitator. Here the setting is much more informal. While the teacher maintains the role of informant, this is a role that can be taken over by any one of the learners at any time. The teacher's main role is to respond to the learners' needs. In this sense the interaction that takes place in the classroom involves all the participants on an equal basis in that anyone can take part as s/he feels inclined to do so. This role is best summed up in the diagram in 4h on page 70. For many people, however, this role is seen as a kind of abdication of the teacher's role and

4g

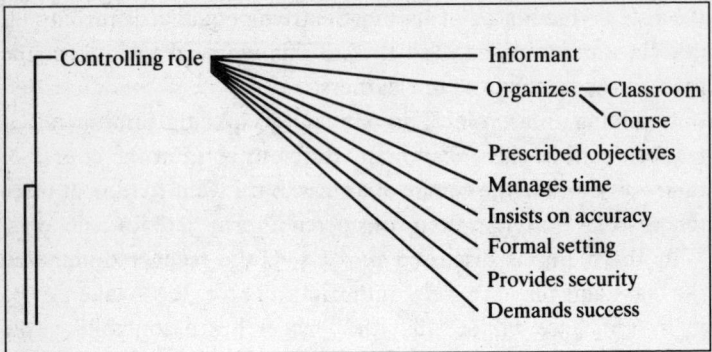

4h

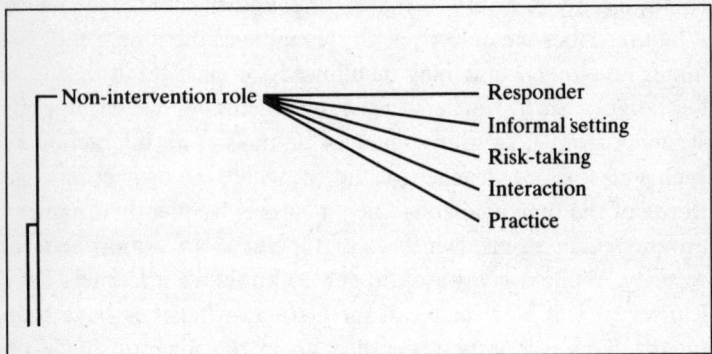

4i

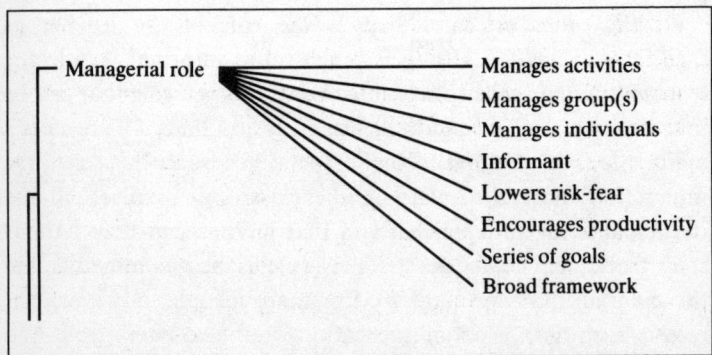

some learners feel insecure when they have taken on so much.

Bell (1984) looks at the role of the teacher as manager. As can be seen in diagram 4i on page 70, here the teacher takes on the role of authority, but is not authoritarian, is responsible for the overall organization of the course and the setting, but encourages learners to become involved. In this way the interaction of the classroom is given a direction provided by the teacher, where the learners feel they are part of the process.

4.2.3 Interactive methodology

With the teacher and the learners all part of the learning process, questions about contextualization and situationalization of grammar exercises take on a different complexion. While the uncontextualized or even vaguely situationalized drill may be unacceptable on its own, it can be placed within a context that is communicative and that encourages communication between learner and learner, and between teacher and learners. Consider the following exercise:

4j
Put the words or phrases in the following sentences in the correct order.
1. David / in a restaurant / eats / often
2. the cinema / Bill / to / goes / never
3. washes / Mary / always / her clothes / Monday morning / on
4. sometimes / they / a holiday / in Wales / have
5. works / Jane / late / often

The problem with this exercise is that learners can sit at their desks to do it. The teacher then reads out the answers and the learners mark their answers correct or incorrect. The whole thing can be done in virtual silence.

71

In a class of twelve-year-olds in Germany, a teacher had written the words or phrases in the exercise in 4j on to cards. Each card had just one word or phrase. The cards with the words from one sentence were put together. The teacher then made several sets of these cards.

The learners were divided into small groups and each group was given a set of the cards. The learners then worked in their groups to make up sentences. In the course of this task there was a lot of discussion about the order in which the words should be put. Thus, there was a lot of interaction going on, although basically it was the same task as that found in the exercise in 4j.

It could be argued that the teacher has become a facilitator here; but I feel the organization of the activity demonstrates much more the role of management.

As a manager, the teacher also takes into account the variables in the Celce-Murcia tables 4d and 4e and other variables, such as age, personality and learning experience.

Age

There is little evidence to suggest that age is a significant factor in our ability to acquire a second language. It should mean that different types of tasks are required. Affective game-type tasks, such as the word-order task above, could be very effective with children and teenagers, whereas adults might find it trivial and want something that 'requires a more cognitive awareness of given rules and the internalization of the rules'.

Personality

Skehan (1989) talks of field-independent (analytical) and field-dependent (holistic) learners – those who like to see how things are built up, and those who are able to take in all the features.

In this case, we are looking at tasks which combine communicative features of interaction with the opportunity to analyse what is taking place within the language.

Learning experience

Many people learning a second or foreign language bring to it attitudes to learning and teaching that have developed from experience at school. From this, they are able to decide what contributes to an appropriate and successful learning experience for them.

What is available for the teacher and the learner? Celce-Murcia also considers ways of focusing on form and compares less effective with more effective ways.

4k

Less effective	More effective
manipulative drills	communicative activities
context-free practice	context-embedded practice
sentence-based exercises	text-based exercises
cognitively undemanding activities	cognitively demanding activities
contrived materials	authentic materials
dull or neutral content	interesting and motivating content

(Celce-Murcia 1985)

This is an interesting chart, and in many ways the right-hand column offers a checklist for evaluating tasks; but it has to be treated with care. For example 'authentic materials' do not always reveal the insights that a cognitively demanding task should. Also, we have to explore the organization of the sentence in order to understand its role in discourse. Finally, in some circumstances manipulative drills are useful if we can develop them within a communicative framework.

It is not easy to identify a communicative activity. No task has a natural intrinsic communicative value. Essentially that quality springs from the relationship that has been established in the classroom between the teacher and the students, and among the students themselves. This applies in both the L1 and L2 classroom.

ACTIVITY

Study table 4l and decide how important you consider each of the items to be in their contribution to your learning.

You have been asked to look at table 4l in very general terms with regard to your experiences of learning. If, however, you had been asked to look at it and consider the items there at three different stages in your life, it may be that there would have been differences in your attitudes at different times. For the young child learning often comes through play. This is part of the process by which children acquire their first language. It is unlikely that children would understand the logic behind any organized syllabus of the kind that underlies most coursebooks. On the other hand, adolescents and adults, whose maturity and learning experience have led them to construct an order in the organization of learning, will be constantly searching for some logical development from one learning unit to the next.

Thus, the interactive nature of a class is itself a variable, which depends on the make-up of the learners and the teacher. The age, personality and experience of both the teacher and the learners are factors that have to be taken into consideration.

4I

	very important	quite important	not important
emotional climate in the classroom			
emotional climate outside			
relevance of topic			
manner of presentation			
richness of context			
the classroom			
classroom activities			
opportunities for self-development			
consciousness-raising activities			
related to other interests			
interaction teacher-student			
interaction student-student			
status of subject			

4.3   Deductive and inductive approaches

There are two approaches to the learning of grammar: one is deductive, i.e. where the teacher explains the rules and meaning to the learner; the other is inductive, where learners are given a lot of examples and establish the rules and meaning for themselves. The examples I have given here are from L2 classes, but in different circumstances they could apply to L1 classes.

4.3.1   Deductive approach

In the deductive class, we would find this kind of situation:

4m
The teacher comes into the class.
Teacher: Today we are going to look at how we can talk about the past.
The teacher writes on the board: Yesterday they play<u>ed</u> in the park.
Teacher: When we want to talk about something in the past, we often add -ed to the verb.
The teacher writes again on the board: Last week I cooked a pie for dinner.

The advantages of this form of teaching is that it offers the learners a clear explanation of the structure and its use; and from the teacher's point of view, it is very time-effective. Many people feel that time needs to be spent on practice and that time spent with problem-solving tasks for learners to discover for themselves is time wasted.

4.3.2 Inductive approach

The argument for inductive learning is that learners become involved in the process of discovering the language and developing their own learning strategies.

In the *Eurolingua* course, cycle 1, unit 5 (for beginners with approximately five hours of English) the students are shown a picture of a living room. Underneath the picture there is a list of the items shown, e.g. *an armchair, a table*, to match to the objects in the picture. Later in the unit, in the grammar section, they are asked to look at the list of words under the picture and devise a rule for the use of 'a' or 'an'.

This type of task involves the learners in the process of language and, as such, Rutherford (1987) claims there is more motivation. Furthermore, if we go back to Fortune's remark on the need for learner training, I think this task helps in this process from the very beginning. It also helps the learner towards what Rubin (1975) says about the good language learner who 'is constantly looking for patterns in the language. He attends to the form in a particular way, constantly analysing, categorizing and synthesizing. He is constantly trying to find schemes for classifying information'.

For many people, the problem with learning a second language is that they have to behave at a level below their intelligence when they use the second language. They don't have the command of the language to be able to say things that they feel intellectually they want to say. This is a very demotivating factor and the reason why so many people who learn the second language as an adolescent or as an adult drop out of class very quickly.

To avoid this, new structures should also be presented within an interesting context. In *Eurolingua* 10, the passive is introduced with a text from the National Trust handbook. Here the

4n

	a) When was the house built?	b) Who was the house owned by?
Bourne Mill	...............1591...............	....
Hughenden Manor	....	....
Hanbury Hall	....	....
Kedlestone Hall	....	....
Moseley Old Hall	....	....

(Littlejohn *et al.* 1993)

presentation combined the learning point with information about Britain, which was of interest to the learners.

After reading the text, the learners have to complete a table (see 4n above) about some English houses, which will lead them into using the passive. The table is based on a problem-solving task, which is based on reading comprehension.

In some ways, here the material is coming close to the demands made by people like Newmark and Reibel. The learner is taken into a situation or a problem and involved in a separate task from that of considering the grammar. Only later is the grammar brought in; this time as if it were a problem-solving task.

4.4 Learner centredness

The advantage of problem-solving tasks, such as those described above, is that they intellectualize the process of learning grammar and allow a focus on form, which is important, while not losing sight of the situation or context.

The focus, however, is not always going to be on form, and the approach needs to continue to the stage where the learners are thinking about use and/or meaning.

In any approach, however, it is important to be aware of how the learners are reacting. Often, one of the problems of the inductive approach to grammar is that the learners feel that they are doing all the work and they want some ideas from the teacher, and they want to know that what they are doing is helping them not only to learn about the language, but also to be able to use the language.

Equally, they might feel that with the deductive approach, they are getting too many lectures from the teacher, which bear little relationship to their needs to be able to use the language.

Experience suggests, therefore, that to take a stand on any one approach will lead to a loss of motivation, and that somewhere we must try to find a way to combine the two or, rather, to create a balance in our classes. The comment made by a television critic in a national British paper, *The Observer*, on a programme about teaching children to read is worth noting here:

It seems that there are two, er, schools of thought on teaching children to read. One believes in drilling them in 'phonics', the sounds of letters. The other school, the campaign for real books, believes that children should learn by reading books.

. . . found a vigorous proponent of each theory and put them into schools where the opposite view prevailed. Of the two, only the phonicator turned out to have a genuinely open mind. The real books man was not for turning. It was all very interesting until one realised that nobody seemed to have considered the idea that perhaps what children need is a combination of the two approaches (*The Observer* 15 August 1993)

Such a balance is important in the teaching of grammar, especially in the presentation stage. During the piloting phase of a recent course book, comments from the teachers piloting the book were that they would like more variation in the ways grammar structures were introduced to the learners. Too much of it was problem-solving.

If the presentation is the time when the organization of the form or the meaning or the use of the structure is made clear to the students, it could be argued that it is the practice itself that reveals this to the students. Furthermore, in adopting a learner-centred approach, one of the tenets is that we should begin where the student is and not stick inflexibly and rigorously to a prescribed approach any more than we would stick inflexibly to the syllabus.

In thinking about presentation and practice, it is not necessarily the case that the former should precede the latter. It may be that it is better to start with a practice task to see if the students need an introduction to the structure and, if they do, what kind of introduction they need. The idea of presentation then practice may not be appropriate. Brumfit (1979) has said that if we adopt a communicative approach, it is something of a contradiction to insist on teacher-led presentations. The situation was often as in 4o, whereas a communicative model might well be like 4p.

4o

present ——————→ drill ——————→ practise in context

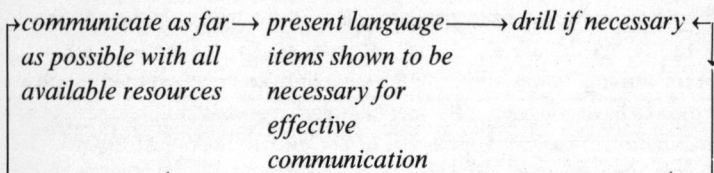

(Brumfit and Johnson 1979)

4p

→communicate as far → present language——→ drill if necessary ←
as possible with all   items shown to be
available resources   necessary for
*   effective*
*   communication*

(Brumfit and Johnson 1979)

If we start from activities that help students to find out what they already know and which help teachers to know what the learners do not know, we are moving closer to a learner-led classroom, which has more relevance to the student-group. The task for the passive described in 4.3.2, based on the National Trust description of English country houses, where the learners need to be able to use the form, is one such. If they can do the task, successfully using the form, there is no need to spend time on it, and the teacher can move on. If they cannot, the teacher is now more clearly aware of what the learners need to know.

This is an approach which applies to both L1 and L2 learning. Also, because the second model begins with a communicative activity, it integrates the teaching of grammar with the development of the use of language. By starting from where the learners are, the syllabus will develop according to the needs of the class and become learner-led.

PROJECT

Devise a lesson plan for teaching a grammar point based on model 4p above. Be clear what your grammar point is and whether you are concerned with form, meaning or use.

SUMMARY

- There have been many approaches and methodologies concerned with the teaching of languages where grammar has been at the centre.
- In deciding what approach to take, it is necessary to take into account learner variables, such as the age, level, purpose and experience of the learner.
- In looking at the 'communicative' approach, we have to consider the role and relationship of the teacher to the learners in the classroom.
- We should aim for an interactive methodology where the learners are involved in the learning process.
- It is better to be eclectic and not be inflexibly wedded to one approach.
- It is important that the learner is at the centre of the classroom experience.

5   Grammar tasks

5.1   Criteria for the selection of tasks

Any methodology is demonstrated by the activities the students
work on in the classroom. It is important that we do not assume
that certain task types are automatically wrong for a particular
method, and equally that we do not assume that others are
appropriate. This chapter looks at criteria for judging tasks, and
describes tasks to help learners become both accurate and fluent
in their use of grammar, while at the same time becoming aware
of the rules that apply.

ACTIVITY

From what you have read so far, and from your personal
experience, what are your criteria for communicative tasks?

One of the casualties of the adoption of the communicative
approach was not simply that, for many people, teaching grammar was seen to be an irrelevance, if not a hindrance, to the
promotion of language learning, but that many exercises and
activities associated with the teaching of grammar were abandoned. In my view, a lot of these, while not being entirely
appropriate, needed development rather than abandonment.

Another unfortunate aspect is the way that communicative
language teaching is seen by some to mean simply putting
together appropriate tasks in the belief that certain tasks are
naturally communicative. Tasks depend for their communicative

quality on the teacher–learner and learner–learner relationships in the classroom. In this way, many traditional tasks can become both communicative and interactive.

I prefer to talk about communicative teaching/learning, omitting the word 'language', as it seems to me that the approach is one that can apply to any subject in the classroom. There is no reason why a Physics or Geography class should not be essentially communicative. Thus the communicative approach is as applicable in the L1 situation as it is in that of the L2.

Perhaps it is also necessary to say that many tasks, by their nature, focus on small areas of grammar and on that structure being used in a sentence. Their purpose is to make the learner aware of how the structure is formed, what it means and how it is used; and to give the learner practice with the structure and the confidence to use it in a larger discourse. The tasks must, therefore, be seen as a means to helping the learner towards greater communicative skills.

In any language classroom, there must be a balance between the focus on specific areas of grammar and the development of communicative competence.

There have been several attempts to set up criteria for communicative tasks. In using these criteria we must look at the outcome of the tasks. It is not possible to do that in a book, since the final judgement will come only when the tasks are used in the classroom. Thus, all I can say here is that the task types below have qualities that promote a communicative teaching/learning situation. Candlin (1987) lists these criteria for communicative tasks:

5a

Tasks should create conditions for:
1. *exploration by the learner of language and language learning;*
2. *challenge and critique by the learner of language, learning and the syllabus;*

3. *negotiations by the learner of language, learning and the syllabus;*
4. *interaction and interdependence among learners and teachers, and among the data, resources and activities of language learning;*
5. *the creating of tactical accounts as a means of evaluating language learning and action and as a means to critiquing curriculum guidelines;*
6. *providing comprehensible input and procedures for engaging that input;*
7. *accommodating differentiation among learners;*
8. *problematicising language, learning and classroom action;*
9. *managing language learning.*

(Candlin and Murphy 1987)

At an in-service course for language teacher trainers in Nijmegen in 1985, the participants came up with the following criteria:

5b

1. BALANCED – *between open-endedness and limited learner resources;*
2. MOTIVATING – *requiring participation, interesting, challenging, regarding, valuable;*
3. CO-OPERATIVE – *developing social and management skills for learning;*
4. STRATEGIC – *stimulating personal strategies for language learning;*
5. DIFFERENTIATED – *varied for different levels, skills, styles, objectives of learners;*
6. FOCUSED – *unambiguous, targeted, relevant to the needs and goals of learners;*
7. OPEN – *extendable, permeable, accessible by/ to learners;*
8. STRUCTURES – *gradable, variable, orderable, organised by learners' time, place and availability;*

9. CRITICAL – *evaluative, formative, offering feedback, problem-posing.*
(Candlin and Murphy 1987)

It is with these conditions in mind that we have to consider the tasks in the two areas of grammar teaching: the input and the practice.

5.2 Input tasks

In some cases, as will be seen later, it is difficult to assign a task to the input phase as opposed to the practice phase. It would be wrong to see the two phases as quite separate and doing totally different things. Rather, the practice phase should be seen as a continuation and development of the input phase. There is no need to feel that everything that has to be learned has to be dealt with in the first phase. Furthermore, if we adopt Brumfit's model (see 4p chapter 4.4), there may be little need on each occasion for an 'input' stage, as such. What may be needed is the fine-tuning that a practice stage gives.

The input phase, however, is where we might say that the focus could be on the teacher. The reason for the modals in that sentence is because I do not want to suggest that the input period should be teacher-dominated. The teacher's role as facilitator and informant apply together with the role of manager.

It is important to remember what Dirven (1990) claims:

The most important requirement of formal grammar teaching and of rule presentations is that they should promote cognitive insight into a given rule and the internalisation of the rule. (Dirven 1990)

For me it is the combination of these two things which unite the input and practice stages and see the one complementing the other.

In chapter 4.3.2, there is an example from the *Eurolingua* course written for EFL students in Switzerland. The task is for beginner learners. What they are being asked to do is to devise a rule based on examples they have been given and then test their hypothesis. To make it interactive the task can easily be done in pairs or small groups.

It can, of course, be argued that at this stage the learners would have very little language at their command to have a proper discussion. This is true. However, they will be able to say something. They will also have a reason for saying something that is authentic. Finally, they will be pushing at their own language barriers. Certainly the task fits in with Dirven's idea of a cognitive task; and to me it is an early task of the kind that Rutherford has called consciousness-raising.

Another important aspect is that from the very beginning, the learners are being put in a position where they are being made responsible for what they can discover about how language is organized. Moreover, it is a task that can be used with adults as well as young learners, and it will draw all kinds of learners into the learning process.

Although the task has been designed for EFL learners, it is equally suitable for children learning about their L1. The methodology would be exactly the same; but, of course, in the L1 situation, the children would have more language at their disposal to express their ideas. Again, it is an important early task, because it is encouraging the learners to think about how they can organize their own knowledge about how language is organized.

If we look at the criteria set out in 5a and 5b above, several of the points are covered. In list 5a:

1. the learner is exploring the language;
2. the learner is involved in developing his/her own learning strategies;

3. the learners' success or otherwise will determine what focus there is on this aspect as they progress through the syllabus;
4. there is interaction and interdependence among the learners;
6. there is comprehensible input and clear procedures;
7. it takes into account the different levels and abilities of the learners;
8. the task is set as a problem;
9. the conditions are there for helping language learning to take place.

From list 5b:

1. it is open-ended and takes account of the learner resources;
2. it requires participation and is challenging and interesting at that level;
3. the group or pair situation develops social and management skills:
4. it lays the ground for learners to think about their own strategies for learning, as well as giving them an example;
5. it is a type of task which can be varied for different levels and approaches to learning;
6. it is clearly focused and is relevant to the learners;
7. it can be extended and developed by the learners;
8. it is a task which can be varied and organized to suit learners' needs and availability;
9. it poses a problem and offers feedback.

ACTIVITY

Consider how you would use the following task from the COBUILD course, then rate it against the criteria in 5a and 5b:

5c

WORDS ENDING IN S

Look at the transcripts below of David and Bridget talking about their families.

How many words are there ending in s or 's?
Does the s or 's always mean the same?

Some words always end in s, for example, <u>his</u>.

What about this one?
<u>I've got one brother and he's got two daughters.</u>

Put the words ending in s or 's into 4 categories.

Bridget's family
DF: *If we look at, erm, your mother Sheila. Has she got any brothers or sisters?*
BG: *Yes, she's got one sister.*
DF: *No brothers?*
BG: *No.*
DF: *Okay. What about your father?*
BG: *He's got three sisters.*
DF: *Oh, and no brothers?*
BG: *No.*

David's family
BG: *Now it's my turn. Your father's called John? and your mother's called Pat? –*
DF: *That's right.*
BG: *and your brother's married – to . . . Jane?*
DF: *Jane. Good.*
BG: *Jane. An they've got two daughters called . . . Emma and – Sarah.*

Now look at the text in section 24. Find thirteen more words that end in s and put them into categories.

(Willis and Willis 1988)

A question that often arises when we are talking about grammar is how much terminology should be learned. While it will not be necessary for learners either of L1 or L2 to know and understand advanced linguistic terminology, it is probably helpful if they understand the kind of terminology that will be found in the contents page of a learner's grammar or EFL course book. Then there is the question of how detailed explanations should be. Very often a limited knowledge of linguistic terminology can make explanations easier.

5.3 Practice tasks

A problem teachers often face is finding suitable tasks for practice purposes.

Teachers need to develop material beyond the coursebook that is of special relevance to their own class or classes. There are already several books which suggest tasks for different grammatical structures, so here I want to give a brief task typology, which for exemplification purposes will use one particular structure, but which could be adapted for other structures. I shall look at five task types:
—traditional with a difference
—affective
—cognitive
—sensitizing
—free tasks

5.3.1 Traditional tasks with a difference

These are tasks which are adaptations of tasks which have been practised for many years. While in themselves the tasks may not provide the right elements for a communicative classroom, they can do so with a slight adjustment or by being given another dimension.

Substitution tables

In the past, substitution tables have often been very dull and led to demotivating repetition, which is often out of context, for example:

5d

I You He She It We They	can	talk walk sing play football

Here, except for the possible choice of 'It' as the subject, the learner will never make a mistake and can make up sentences from the table without even thinking about what they mean.

However, a variation on that can provide learners with more to do and at the same time practise a grammatical point:

5e

Read the following and make grammatically correct statements, using the chart below, to describe <u>vertical people</u> and <u>horizontal people</u>.

Mark your statements V for vertical people and H for horizontal people. Choose only statements that you believe to be true from the information you have in the text. You will not need to use all the sentences possible from the chart. An example has been written for you.

Example:

They need to learn Russian. (V)

Jill Tweedie divides the world into two types of people – vertical people and horizontal people. Vertical people are those who feel pressure to do things and need things to change. What's new? they ask. What's next? They're always planning to do things. Their lives are full of 'needs' and 'musts'. Having another baby; writing a new book; travelling to a new country: they're always trying to get involved in new things. Horizontal people, on the other hand, feel none of these pressures. They are content with a comfortable life. What's your next step? Where do you plan to go? you ask them. Nowhere, they reply. We just want more of the same.

	must	
	don't have to	*lose weight*
	should	*get a new partner*
	couldn't	*to learn Russian*
	could	*be content*
They	*need*	*own a house*
	needn't	*look at the garden*
	can	*to have a baby*
	mustn't	*have nice children*
	can't	*cut the grass*
	don't need	*change jobs*
	have to	

(Woods and McLeod 1990: 2.26)

In this task, we have the basic substitution table, but the learners have to do more than just make correct form sentences. They are also involved in reading comprehension and discussion. In this way, the practice of a grammatical point becomes part of a discussion about the topic. The task is interactive and at the same time the grammar point is being put into a context. In this way it is practising both form and meaning.

The text in the task is clearly for a more advanced class, but simpler ones can be found for beginner and lower intermediate classes.

Another common use of the substitution table idea for an early class is one where the learners write their own.

Survey chart

Another well-tried task is the use of a table for the simple present or frequency adverbs. This is often based on a story made up by the teacher or coursebook writer. Even when it is based on a real event, it is something given to the learners.

A simple adaptation would be for the learners to do a survey about what people do and how often things are done. This can be conducted either in the class among themselves or in an L1 class, or in the area where they live. When they have completed the survey, each learner has to write a short report or give an oral presentation saying what has been discovered from the survey. In this example not only is the grammar structure being practised, but it is also being integrated into the practice of other communicative skills.

Gap-filling

Another task is one based on gap-filling, where the learners are given an incomplete table and asked to complete it from accompanying information. Such a task can be adapted to create more learner involvement, as in the task here. This task, which is to give practice with the comparison of adjectives, is in three stages. In the first stage, the learners have to complete the table by reading the text:

5f

Around Britain

	Sun hrs	Rain in	Max C	F	
Falmouth	6.2	–	20	68	sunny
Penzance	6.0	–	20	68	bright
Scilly Isles	3.6	–	18	64	sunny
Jersey	3.0	–	19	66	cloudy
Guernsey	5.5	–	19	66	sunny
Newquay	(a)	.02	19	66	sunny
Ilfracombe	*	.02	*	*	sunny
Minehead	7.8	.01	20	68	sunny
B'pool Airpt	5.7	–	17	63	bright
Morecambe	8.5	–	17	63	sunny
Douglas	*	–	17	63	sunny
(b)	4.5	–	22	72	sunny
Leeds	6.0	–	21	70	sunny
Nottingham	2.3	–	21	70	cloudy
(c)	3.3	–	19	66	bright
(d)	4.5	–	15	59	sunny
(e)	5.8	.02	17	63	bright
Aviemore	4.7	–	17	63	cloudy
Kinloss	7.3	–	19	66	sunny
(f)	8.1	.02	15	59	sunny
Stornoway	4.7	.01	16	61	shower
Tiree	7.5	.01	16	61	bright
(g)	5.7	.03	17	63	shower

* Denotes figures not available

(Woods and McLeod 1990: 4.2)

Complete the chart from the information given in the text below.

The hottest place in Britain yesterday was Birmingham Airport, which recorded a temperature of 22°C. The lowest recorded temperature was 15°C in Colwyn Bay and Lerwick. Tenby had a higher temperature than Colwyn Bay, but it was colder there than it was at Anglesey. However, Anglesey had fewer hours of sunshine than Colwyn Bay, although throughout the day, it was hotter. The sunniest place in Britain was Newquay with 11.2 hours of sunshine. Wick had the most rain. It was warmer there than at Colwyn Bay, which had no rain at all; but it was colder than in Jersey, although it was sunnier than in Jersey.

In stage two the learners are given a similar chart on which they have to blank out certain pieces of information of their own choosing, then write a text similar to that accompanying the first chart. In this way, they have developed a task similar to the one they themselves did in stage one:

5g

Write a text similar to the one in Stage One, using the chart below.

Abroad

MIDDAY: *t = thunder; d = drizzle; fg = fog; s = sun*
sl = sleet; sn = snow; f = fair; c = cloud; r = rain

	C	F		C	F
Ajaccio	28	82 s	Budapest	23	73 c
Akrotiri	29	84 s	B Aires	14	57 s
Alex'dria	31	88 f	Cairo	34	94 s
Algiers	31	88 s	Cape Tn	13	55 c
Amst'dam	17	63 c	C'blanca	25	77 s
Athens	33	91 s	Chicago	25	77 c
Bahrain	35	95 s	Ch'church	7	45 c
Barcelna	24	75 f	Cologne	22	72 f
Belgrade	25	77 s	C'phagn	19	66 f

	C	F		C	F
Berlin	22	72 c	Corfu	32	90 s
Bermuda	31	88 s	Dublin	17	63 f
Biarritz	19	66 c	Dubrovnik	30	86 s
Borde'x	22	72 f	Faro	25	77 s
Brussels	17	63 c	Florence	32	90 s

(Woods and McLeod 1990: 4.2)

The final stage is when the learners give the task they have developed to other learners. This gives yet more practice and also checks that the text they have written themselves is appropriate.

There is nothing very original about the basic task here. The advantage of the three stages is that it allows a lot of practice on a very small point, which is often necessary, but requires some kind of variation. It also involves the learners in the development of their own learning by having them produce a task which is then given to other learners to do.

5.3.2 Affective tasks

'Affective' is the name I give to tasks which give the learners, especially young learners, some kind of fun outside the world of language learning. Usually such tasks are based on games.

We have already seen in chapter 4.2.3 how a word-order task can be changed into something communicative. Another way of doing this is the following task:

In the first task the learners must see how many sentences they can make using the imperative form. The learners are

TASK ONE

Work round the circle below as often as you like and see how many correctly formed imperatives you can find. You must keep the words in the order you find them. You can start at any point in the circle.

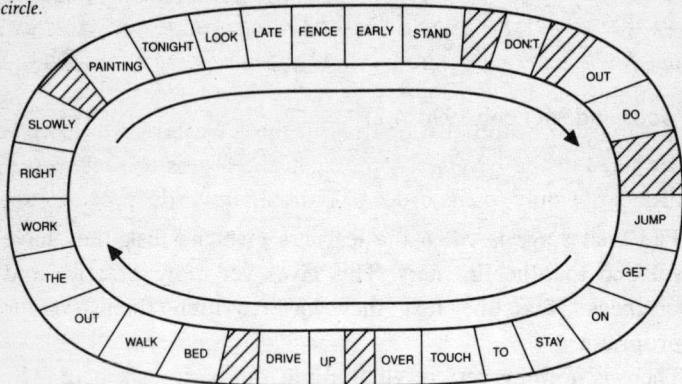

TASK TWO

Now fit the imperatives you have found in TASK ONE with the pictures below.

(Woods & McLeod 1992 : 1.4)

divided into small groups so they can discuss the sentences as they move round the circle. There can also be some kind of competition among the groups to see who can make the most sentences.

In the second task, the learners have the opportunity to check what they have done and relate their sentences to another situation.

Such a task could also be used in the L1 classroom and at a later stage in the L2 classroom, when the aim is to sensitize the learners not only to the order of individual words in a sentence, but to the general organization of complex sentences and sentences within a discourse.

Both of the tasks are concerned with practice with form, so they can be used at a very elementary level. Variations are available for more advanced levels.

Games themselves can be adapted: Rinvolucri (1984) adapts the game of Monopoly for practising different tenses; Ur (1988) shows how memory games can be used for practising countable and unaccountable nouns; and Brumfit & Windeatt (1983) make use of several problem-solving tasks.

Most of the affective task types are useful for giving further practice with form. The advantage of many of them is that they will give the learners the opportunity to monitor themselves, be it in L1 or L2.

ACTIVITY

Think of a game you know and see how you could adapt it for practising a grammar point.

5.3.3 Cognitive tasks

While it is possible to give learners a lot of opportunities to practise without focusing on the rules behind the structure, there are occasions where it might be better to put the focus on the rules. This is especially the case when the structure is one that is not used in the same way in the learner's L1, or where the structure might not even exist. Such is the case with the article.

For some learners its use in English is confused with its use in their L1; for others, it is a feature of language that does not exist in their L1, as in Turkish or Japanese.

Some teachers feel that overtly drawing the learners' attention to the rules of a language is to draw attention away from the use of a language. As learners become more advanced in their knowledge of the language, the two – rules and use – could complement each other. For example, with the article we might have a task such as 5i, in which learners are asked to fill in the blanks in a text with 'the', 'a' or 'an', or 0 if there should be no article. This task would then be complemented with one in which learners read several passages, of which 5j is an example, underline all the examples of 'the', then write the examples in a chart.

ACTIVITY

How would you measure these tasks against the criteria in 5.1?

5i

..... *National Trust is to spend £12.5m over ..... next four years on ..... conservation and restoration in ..... Lake District, ... national park. Launching ..... public appeal for £2m recently, ... Trust said that growing pressures on ..... area posed ..... severe financial problems. With ..... area of only just over 880 square miles ..... Lake*

District attracted ..... 1 million visitors ..... year with inevitable pressures on ..... parking facilities ..... woods and hedgerows, ... habitats for many of ..... rare animals and flora of ..... Lakes, were being lost.
(Woods and McLeod 1990: 3.4)

5j

Various people have managed to sell <u>the</u> Eiffel Tower over the years, but nobody has managed to steal the thing itself. In Uruguay the police are on the trail of the first burglar-engineers who sound capable of going for the big one. They unbolted the 160ft-long iron bridge over the river Santa Lucia Chico in the town of Florida, and removed it overnight. No one is quite sure how, or what they have done with it.

Mentioned before	Specified in the noun group	By context	
		Local	Global
			the Eiffel Tower

(Woods and McLeod 1990: 3.4)

The second task gives the learner the opportunity to see why the uses of the article were such in the first task, without the need for the teacher to explain. Again it is consciousness-raising.

Such tasks are also useful when thinking of how to help learners with understanding the terminology. It may not always be appropriate for learners to know the terminology; but in some cases it is, with the L2 as well as the L1.

In the same way, pairing is useful because it helps learners to develop their own cognitive skills in analysing grammar and articulating how it works.

The aim of a cognitive task is to enable learners to make themselves conscious of how grammar works and the context in which it is operating.

5.3.4   Sensitizing tasks

Although many grammar books like to present strong prescribed rules for every aspect of grammar, there are areas of
grammar where it is not possible to give exact prescribed rules
for use. Take, for example, the difference between the use of the
present perfect and the present perfect continuous in these
examples:

I've been waiting here for over an hour.
I've waited here for over an hour.

The choice the speaker makes here is determined by his/her
attitude to the event and it is not a question of when the event
took place or the length of time of the event. Thus, tasks need to
be found which make the learner aware of this fact rather than
trying to explain in precise detail.

Even when there is a more obvious distinction in meaning
and/or use, a sensitizing task can give the learner a feel for the
language. It is part of developing a sense of language awareness
in the learner.

In Woods and McLeod (1990), there is a task where the
learners are given a series of pictures showing students doing
typical things, such as working late, going to the disco, having
late-night conversations with friends, attending lectures, and so
on. The rubric for the task is:

5k
*After the spring vacation, Barbara and John will be going back to
university and getting back into the same routine as before the
holidays. Write some sentences, using will/shall or 'll + be continuous infinitive about what they will be doing when they get
back. Use the cues (pictures) to help you or think up your own
activities.*
(Woods and McLeod 1990: 2.11)

After they have done that task, there is a second part:

5l

If you rewrote the sentences using be going to + infinitive, how would the meaning of the statements change?
(Woods and McLeod 1990: 2.11)

The exercise below comes in a unit looking at the passive and at feature articles in newspapers.

5m

Look at the following text and decide if it is suitable for inclusion in the features page of a newspaper. In some cases, it may be better to use the passive form. You don't have to make any changes, but if you do, you must give reasons for doing so.

> *If it is true that one can tell an area from its notice-boards, then one can easily find out if one would like to live there. Of course one has to interpret the messages very carefully, and also consider them as a whole. This is necessary in order to avoid the situation where a minor piece of information can take you in, although it isn't representative of the notices as a whole. Equally one should not totally ignore the unusual notice, since this may herald a new trend in the area. While it is true that one swallow doesn't make a summer, one should remember that a change has to start somewhere. Often this affects older districts which people have neglected and allowed to run down. Suddenly because these are often quite cheap areas to live in, some young people move and this starts to change the district.*

After the text there is a box divided vertically into two. On one side learners write the changes to be made, and on the other their reasons for the changes.

What should be noticed in this task is that the learners don't have to change anything into the passive, but where they do make changes, they have to find reasons for doing so. It is open and free, and what the teacher is interested in is the reasons given.

Such tasks as those above help learners to explore the language for themselves and develop an awareness of how the language is used. I shall look very briefly at language awareness in the next chapter.

5.3.5   Free tasks

By the term 'free tasks', I do not mean tasks that are concerned only with general communication, but tasks which, while focusing on a particular area of grammar, give the learners greater freedom to express themselves.

The following are examples of this:

5n

Look at all the written work you have done in your English class and find out what kind of errors you have made. Then write a report saying which are your most frequent errors and which your least frequent ones, comparing the different types of errors you have made and, if possible, giving reasons for the errors. An example has been written for you.

Example:

I have looked at six essays and six grammar tasks. I made more errors in the essays than in the grammar tasks because the latter are easier to do correctly.

(Woods and McLeod 1990: 3.11)

5o

Think of six newspaper headlines for good news that you would like to have happen. Then join with another person and discuss what the story might be. Choose one of your partner's headlines and write the story.

Examples:

NEW VACCINE ELIMINATES ALL VIRUSES
WAR ABOLISHED
FREE BOOKS FOR E.F.L. LEARNERS

And here is an example of one of the stories:

> *The EC has announced that all charges for books for registered EFL learners have been abolished. The publishers have agreed to supply free books to anyone who has enrolled in a full- or part-time English course and the EC members have promised to subsidise this enterprise. Commenting on the announcement, Ralph Marsh of the British Council said, 'I think they have made a very wise decision'. A student in Kuala Lumpur said, 'I have spent many hundreds of ringgit on books for my studies. Last month I spent fifty ringgit on a new dictionary and my teacher has told me that I need a new grammar book. Now I can get all the books I want'.*

(Woods and McLeod 1990: 2.17)

These tasks need to be monitored very carefully; but they allow learners greater freedom of expression.

Willis and Willis (1988) discuss an interesting task which is basically a communicative activity, but which features a clear focus on grammar.

In the first stage the students, in groups, are given a problem to solve. In the final stage each group has to report on how they solved the problem.

The middle stage is the one that focuses on grammar. One student in each group is designated to give the final report, but the whole group is involved in its preparation. The authors claim that because the report is to be made in public the learners will take care in the preparation of the report to make sure the grammar is correct and this will promote discussion about the grammar to be used. What the teacher has to be careful about is that a structure is not forced into a situation.

Dean (1993) has an interesting use of poetry:

5p

A POEM KIT

'will' for predicting
Work in pairs or groups. Write four sentences then start with 'When I'm old I'll . . .'. Cut or tear the paper so that there is only one sentence on each piece of paper. Pass the pieces of paper around until each pair or group has four sentences that they did not write. Rewrite the sentences as a four-sentence poem. Only the first line has 'when I'm old . . .'. The other three lines start with 'I'll'. The poem does not have to rhyme but read the lines aloud for a good rhythm. Here is an example:

> *When I'm old I'll have cornflakes for tea (no teeth you know).*
> *I'll walk carefully.*
> *I'll be happy, you'll see.*
> *I'll play music for you and me.*

Still talking about the future, he has a task which gets learners involved in their environment by planning what they will do about their classroom or their town. Such planning activities can also be used to practise the use of modals such as *could* and *might*.

Finally, it has to be remembered that tasks in the main focus on particular structures. The next stage is to see how students use the language in longer discourse, such as in discussion or in essays. It is also important to remember that while at one level concern may be for accurate use of grammar, teachers should not fall into the trap of looking at low-level syntax (see 1.3.2), but should concern themselves with trying to tease out what the student is trying to express and then try to find the best way to express the idea. In this way we are approaching grammar according to Halliday's idea that we should not try to find out what this form means, but how best we can express what we want to say. Thus, our focus has moved from form to language awareness, which is where we want our students to be.

SUMMARY

- Grammar tasks need to involve learners in a cognitive process.
- In developing appropriate tasks, it is necessary to work with a set of criteria against which the task can be measured.
- There will be different approaches to tasks depending on whether the teacher is dealing with something new, either form or use, or whether it is a session for further practice.
- We should not abandon the more traditional tasks, but see how they can be developed and made interactive and cognitive.
- Tasks must involve the learners and at the same time direct them to a greater awareness of how language is used.

6 Language awareness

6.1 What is language awareness?

The tasks in the previous chapter give the student the opportunity to internalize and use structures correctly in their form and, in a general sense, in their meaning and use. They promote an active methodology where the student is interacting with colleagues while at the same time teasing out the correct form and the proper use.

Alongside all this, however, it is necessary to add a more conscious, analytic dimension if we are to achieve the final goal of the syllabus proposed at the end of chapter 3, i.e. language awareness.

What is 'language awareness'? It can mean different things to different people, especially when we look at its role in the classroom. On the one hand, the aim is to give learners an approach to looking at how language is used in a functional way. On the other hand, it is considered to be the tool which empowers people to unwrap the covert messages within an utterance or piece of writing.

Why does the journalist use the passive in the newspaper report in chapter 2.4? Why has the copywriter moved the prepositional phrase to the front of the sentence in the advertisement described in chapter 1.2.4?

For detailed work on language awareness, Hawkins (1984), Fairclough (1990), Fowler (1991) and James and Garrett (1991) are a few of the writers who have contributed in this field, building on the earlier work of Halliday, Kress and Fowler.

More recently, for classroom work, Tomlinson (1994) has some interesting tasks linked to texts helping learners to develop such strategies. Wright (1994) provides a lot of ideas useful for both teachers and learners.

6.2 Why is language awareness important?

In a society where the main form of communication is through language, in order to understand fully and interpret properly the messages that are conveyed to us, and in order to communicate our own ideas successfully, it is important that we understand how language is and can be used both functionally and to convey meaning. I would go as far as to say that democracy only survives when people understand how language is being used in the messages delivered to them through the media and by politicians. This is not suggesting there is any dishonesty, but to state that in our societies, language is the principal tool by which people are persuaded and manipulated. The persuasion and manipulation may be good for society as a whole. It is important, nonetheless, that people are aware of it.

As stated above, in chapters 1 and 2, there are examples of how journalists and advertising copywriters can organize language to promote their messages effectively.

This is not to advocate that the grammar class should be opened up to political propagandizing. On the contrary, my concern is only that people are aware of how messages are constructed and what that signifies.

Language awareness involves more than just grammar. Lexical selection is equally important. For the purposes of this chapter, however, I want to concentrate solely on the grammatical aspects.

Language awareness is not something that has been hitherto ignored in the classroom. Many grammar books in the past have included it in some way. As far back as 1856 in *An English Grammar for the Use of Schools* there were exercises on style, which were concerned with helping the learner to use language effectively.

Language awareness in the classroom is, however, more than this. It is concerned with looking not at the accuracy of the use of the language, which will be taken for granted, but looking at how the language has been used by the speaker or writer to focus the message, to determine one interpretation where there might be several, or even to encourage a particular emotional response.

In his review of the film 'Reds', Derek Malcolm has continually used words and phrases that are very positive:

6a

Most intelligent . . . amazing what a good job . . . it has the courage to ask . . . If romance it is, at least it is a very good one, about interesting people and set against stirring and fascinating times . . . the whole thing is linked and underscored by the most audacious and, as it turns out, successful device . . . squinting at Vittorio Sotraro's eloquent camera . . . 'Reds' does make history more watchable and more involving . . . what it remains is something very definitely to see.
(*Guardian* 7 March 1982)

The effect of so many phrases of this nature is to give the reader a very positive feeling about the film.

Repetition of this kind can be used for both positive and negative effects and can work at a very emotional level.

6.3   Language awareness in the classroom

The process of awareness-raising is seen as a gradual one. Attitudes and beliefs change slowly – language awareness is concerned, therefore, with behavioural outcomes rather than products, *per se*. The outcomes are associated with changes of attitude, greater insight, and the foundations for future courses of action. (Wright and Bolitho, 1993)

It is important to highlight the point about outcomes. Language awareness is not a matter of the teacher telling the student what is right and what is wrong; it is rather a process by which the learner comes to examine the language that is used. Learners must find their own way through this process. They must be made aware that there are no definitive answers.

In Woods and McLeod there is task which is based on a text advising people going abroad what they need to do about travel documents and health protection. It is an authentic text containing many modal verbs. These have been deleted and the learners have to complete the text. For example:

6b
Find out about the health risks in the country you are visiting, and the precautions you . . . take, by reading the chart on page 5.
(Woods and McLeod 1990)

It is possible for learners to choose different modals here, *can*, *must*, *should* etc., any of which would be correct. It is not important that they should choose the same modal as the one used in the original text. Where they have chosen an alternative which is acceptable, they have to justify their own choice. In this way, they can show that they understand the difference between the modals in their meaning and use.

Texts are not always what they seem. In 1980, a British newspaper published a travel article about Berlin. The text begins:

6c
Scattered below London are about a dozen abandoned stations, the casualties of planning. As the train rattles past, alert passengers can see their stripped-down shells.

Underneath Berlin are also a dozen abandoned stations, but these are casualties of ideology. (*Sunday Telegraph* 30 March 1980)

On the surface, this is a feature about what to do during a weekend break in Berlin in the 1980s before the reunification of Germany, but the writer has used the article to express a dislike of certain aspects of Germany (both East and West) and the Communist system.

As far as grammar is concerned, it is interesting here to see how the writer has made use of participle adjuncts. The parallelism in the structure of the opening two paragraphs helps to set the tone showing an abhorrence of 'ideology'. The lexical choice reflected in 'scattered below' being opposed by 'underneath' helps to highlight this abhorrence, but the effect would surely be less if these adjuncts were placed at the end of their respective sentences:

6d
—*There are about a dozen abandoned tube stations, the casualties of planning scattered below London . . .*
—*There are also a dozen abandoned stations underneath Berlin . . .*

A lot of students, both L1 and L2, are taught correctly that adjuncts such as these can come either at the end or the beginning of a sentence. They understand there is a choice, but the significance of the choice is not often made clear.

In order to help students become aware of this significance, it is necessary to develop the kind of sensitizing tasks discussed in chapter 5, and give them more analytical tasks to do. Here is one task for examining the text of the article 'Berlin beckons':

6e
—*In your groups make a list of where the author uses this marked feature of adjuncts.*
—*Rewrite the sentences in the more conventional S–V–O order.*

—Discuss the effects the author's use has on your interpretation of the passage.

This is the fourth in a series of tasks, which examine what the author was saying.

The first two tasks help to draw the learner's attention to what is actually in the text by way of information. This is a travel article, so we might expect to find a lot of facts about the city. The third task looks at the lexis used and is an attempt to sensitize the learners about lexis and what it can convey. The fourth and final task examines the way the grammar is used.

ACTIVITY

Measure the task for 'Berlin beckons' in 6e, above, by the criteria set out in chapter 5.1.

What is important here, and in any language awareness task, is that the learners are examining the text for themselves and drawing their own conclusions about how the language has been used and what it conveys to them.

It is an important development for L1 learners to have complete control of their language and for L2 learners to become proficient in their use of the language.

The work in this chapter is for higher-level learners, both native speakers and second language learners. It is important, however, that language awareness is not seen to be only for those learners who get to an advanced stage; similar work relating to grammar can be developed at a fairly early stage.

This kind of work depends on the texts available. In reaction to Celce-Murcia's table of appropriate ways to focus on grammar (see 4.2.3), I spoke cautiously about using authentic texts. In the case of language awareness, however, it is important that such texts are used. They do not have to be long and literary. Such work can be done with texts of only one, two or three sentences, such as found in advertisements or comic strips. You could, for example, devise a task like the one above using the two advertisements in chapter 1.2.5. Work of this nature is an essential part of the process as we move up the scale from form through meaning and use.

ACTIVITY

Devise a task for your learners based on the two advertisements (chapter 1.2.5) or on the newspaper articles (chapter 2.4).

Language awareness is much more than I have dealt with in this short chapter and another book in this series will look at it in greater detail. My aim has been to show that it is a part of 'grammar teaching' and that analytical tasks of the kind shown above are also a part of learning grammar, which helps learners reflect on how language is used.

SUMMARY

- 'language awareness' is an understanding of how language is used and an ability to make appropriate choices in our own use of language. It is important because language is a very powerful tool which can be used to inform and persuade people.
- While grammar is only one aspect of language awareness, learners should understand its importance in helping us to focus and convey our messages.
- Both L1 and L2 learners need opportunities to explore and analyse how language is used.
- Language awareness is an important end-goal in language teaching.

Further reading

Bolinger, D. 1977. *Meaning and Form*. Harlow: Longman.
An interesting book arguing that the choices that are available to the speaker affect the message being conveyed. After the first general chapter, the chapters look at specific grammatical points.

Carter, R. (ed.) 1990. *Knowledge about Language and the Curriculum*. London: Hodder and Stoughton.
A collection of articles about language in the British National Curriculum. Chapter 5 looks at Grammar.

Celce-Murcia, M. (ed.) 1991. *Teaching English as a Second or Foreign Language*. New York: Newbury House.
The chapter on Teaching Grammar details Larsen-Freeman's 'pie' model.

Chalker, S. 1984. *Current English Grammar*. Basingstoke: Macmillan.
A very useful and insightful grammar book for students and teachers.

Cox, B. 1991. *Cox on Cox*. London: Hodder and Stoughton.
Cox argues his case for the recommendations of the national Curriculum English Working Group. Chapter 4 discusses Grammar in the Classroom.

eastLINC 1991. *Looking at Grammar*. eastLINC Consortium.
A handbook of papers discussing the teaching of grammar and its integration with speaking and writing.

Halliday, M.A.K. 1985. *An Introduction to Functional Grammar*. London: Edward Arnold.
A readable account of the theory of systemic grammar, but looking at how language is used and how and why choices are made.

Leech, G. *et al.* 1982. *English Grammar for Today*. Basingstoke: Macmillan.
A practical and useful analysis of grammar, written for use in British schools and universities.

Richards, J.C. 1985. *The Context of Language Teaching*. Cambridge, C.U.P.

A collection of papers on language teaching, with some useful chapters on grammar and some practical examples for teaching.

Rutherford, W.F. 1987. *Second language Grammar – learning and teaching*. Harlow: Longman.

An important book setting out Rutherford's ideas for a consciousness-raising approach to teaching/learning grammar.

Stern, H.H. 1992. *Issues and Options in Language Teaching*. Oxford: Oxford University Press.

A collection of papers analysing current issues in language teaching. Chapter 5 looks at Grammar and the syllabus.

Willis, D. 1990. *The Lexical Syllabus*. Glasgow: Collins COBUILD.

Willis sets out his ideas for the lexical syllabus. Particularly interesting because it is told against a background account of the development of the syllabus for the COBUILD course.

Wright, T. 1994. *Investigating English*. London: Edward Arnold.

A book of activities for both teachers and learners to increase their awareness of how English is used.

Glossary

behaviourist approach An approach to language learning, associated with the Direct method, whereby learners were given lots of drills to practise a structure, often out of any context.

communicative competence The ability to use language correctly, selectively and appropriately on each occasion.

consciousness-raising The process by which learners are made aware of the structure of a language. This is achieved by providing tasks which not only make them aware of this but also help them to make comparisons with the structures of their own language.

deixis The use of words that point or indicate, such as the demonstratives (*this*, *that*, *these,, those*), the articles and personal pronouns.

discourse analysis The analysis of language *in use*, looking at a broader framework than the sentence or clause and going across such boundaries.

EFL The abbreviation for English as a Foreign Language, i.e. where it is taught as a school subject. It is not normally a medium of instruction, nor is it used for communication in business, law, politics, etc.

interlanguage Stages in learning a second or foreign language where the learner mixes his accurate knowledge of the target language with hypotheses based on that knowledge and on comparisons with the mother tongue.

L1 The learner's first or native language or mother tongue.

L2 The target language that the learner is learning.

morpheme The parts of a word that convey meaning. In the analysis of word structure a contrast is made between units that can stand alone and those that cannot. For example, in 'walked' there are two morphemes: 'walk', which can stand alone and is 'free', and '-ed', which cannot stand alone and is 'bound'. Morphemes need no grammatical status (unless the syllable is identical to a morpheme).

pragmatics The study of how people use language to convey what they want to say in the context of the situation, e.g. It's cold in here' could be a simple statement of fact or a request to have the door or window closed.

semantics The formal meanings expressed in a language without reference to the context.

SLA Second language acquisition. The study of how people learn or acquire a second language.

substitution tables A type of exercise for practising the correct grammatical forms, especially associated with the Direct Method and oral approach method.

suffix A morpheme that can be added to the end of a word, e.g. '-ment'.

syntax the organization of words in a clause or sentence – grammar as form.

usage Using language to show a grammatical knowledge of the language or to give an example of the correct grammatical form, and not for a communicative purpose.

use Using language to communicate ideas and messages in a real context.

References

Abbs, B., A. Ayton and **I. Freebairn.** 1975. *Strategies.* Harlow: Longman.

Adamson, D. and **D. Cobb.** 1987. *Active Grammar Exercises.* Harlow: Longman.

Anderson, J. 1971. *The Grammar of Case.* Cambridge: Cambridge University Press.

Bell, R. 1984. Classroom management – a gallon in a pint pot. *System* Vol. 12, No. 2. Oxford: Pergamon Press.

Bolinger, D. 1977. *Meaning and Form.* London: Longman.

Bosewitz, R. 1987. *Penguin Students' Grammar of English.* London: Penguin.

Brumfit, A. and **S. Windeatt.** 1983. *Communicative Grammar.* Beirut: ELTA/Oxford: Oxford University Press.

Brumfit, C. 1979. 'Communicative' language teaching – an educational perspective. In C. Brumfit and K. Johnson (eds.) *The Communicative Approach to Language Teaching.* Oxford: Oxford University Press.

Brumfit, C. 1981. Teaching the 'general' student. In K. Johnson and K. Morrow (eds.) *Communication in the Classroom – applications and methods for a communicative approach.* Harlow: Longman.

Bruton, A. 1984. Language learning strategies – a case study. *Modern English Teacher* Vol. 12, No. 2.

Canale, M. and **M. Swain.** 1980. Theoretical bases of communicative approaches to second language teaching and testing. *Applied Linguistics* Vol. 1, No. 1.

Candlin, C. 1987. Towards task-based language learning. In C. Candlin and D. Murphy (eds.) *Lancaster Practical Papers in English Language Education ' – language learning tasks.* London: Prentice Hall.

Carter, R. A. 1991. *The national curriculum for English – a guide to the* *development of a national curriculum for English in England and Wales.* London: British Council.

Carter, R. 1993. *Introducing Applied Linguistics.* London: Penguin.

Celce-Murcia, M. 1985. Making informed decisions about the role of grammar in language teaching. *TESOL Newsletter* Vol. 19, No. 1.

Chalker, S. 1984. *Current English Grammar.* Basingstoke: Macmillan.

Close, R. A. 1981. *English as a Foreign Language – its constant grammatical problems.* London: Allen and Unwin.

Cobbett, W. 1819. *A Grammar of the English Language.* Oxford: Oxford University Press. (New edition published 1984.)

Collins COBUILD. 1990. *Collins COBUILD English Grammar.* London: Collins.

Cook, V. 1991. *Second Language Learning and Language Teaching.* London: Edward Arnold.

Corder, S. P. 1967. The significance of learners' errors. *IRAL* Vol. 5, No. 1, Heidelberg: Julius Groos Verlag.

Dean, M. 1993. *English Grammar Lessons.* Oxford: Oxford University Press.

Dirven, R. 1990. State of the art: pedagogical grammar. CILT Vol. 23, No. 1.

Dulay, H. C. and **M. Burt.** 1974. Natural sequence in child second language. *Language Learning*, 24.

eastLINC. 1991. Looking at grammar. Language In the Curriculum project. EastLINC consortium.

Eisenstein, M. 1987. Grammatical explanations in ESL – teach the student not the method. In M. Long and J. Richards (eds.) *Methodology in TESOL – a book of readings.* Rowley, Mass.: Newbury House.

Ellis, R. 1993. The structural syllabus and second language acquisition. TESOL Quarterly, 27, 1.

Fairclough, N. (ed.) 1990. *Critical Language Awareness.* Harlow: Longman.

Fortune, A. 1992. Self-study grammar practice: learners' views and preferences. *ELT Journal*, Vol. 46, No. 2.

Fowler, R. 1991. *Language in the News.* London: Routledge.

References

Givón, T. 1979. *On Understanding Grammar*. London: Academic Press.

Halliday, M. A. K. 1985. *An Introduction to Functional Grammar*. London: Edward Arnold.

Harmer, J. 1987. *Teaching and learning Grammar*. Harlow: Longman.

Hartley, B. and P. Viney. 1978. *Streamline English – Departures*. *Oxford: Oxford University Press*.

Hawkins, E. 1984. *Awareness of Language – an introduction*. Cambridge: Cambridge University Press.

Huddleston, R. 1988. *English Grammar – an outline*. Cambridge: Cambridge University Press.

Hudson, R. 1992. *Teaching Grammar – a guide for the national curriculum*. Oxford: Basil Blackwell.

Hymes, D. H. 1971. On communicative competence. In J. B. Pride and J. Holmes (eds.) 1972. *Sociolinguistics – selected readings*. London: Penguin.

James, C. and P. Garrett. (eds.) 1991. *Language awareness in the Classroom*. Harlow: Longman.

Johnson, K. 1978. Syllabus design and the adult beginner. *Modern English Teacher* Vol. 6, No. 2.

Johnston, M. 1985. Second language acquisition research in the adult migrant education program. *Prospect* Vol. 1, No. 1.

Krashen, S. and T. D. Terrell. 1983. *The Natural Approach – language acquisition in the classroom*. Oxford: Pergamon Press.

Larsen-Freeman, D. 1991. Teaching grammar. In M. Celce-Murcia (ed.) 1991. *Teaching English as a Second or Foreign Language*. New York: Newbury House.

Leech, G., M. Deuchar and R. Hoogenraad. 1982. *English Grammar for Today*. Basingstoke: Macmillan.

Leech, G. and J. Svartvik. 1975. *A Communicative Grammar of English*. London: Longman.

Littlejohn, A. *et al.* 1993. *Eurolingua*. Zurich: FMC-Coordination Office of the Club Schools.

Littlewood, W. 1981. *Communicative Language Teaching – an introduction*. Cambridge: Cambridge University Press.

National Curriculum Council. 1990. National curriculum non-statutory guidance – modern foreign languages for ages 11–16. Welsh Office: Department for Education.

National Education in Ireland. 1856. An English grammar for the use of schools. Dublin: Commissioners of National Education in Ireland.

Newmark, L. 1963. Grammatical theory and the teaching of English as a foreign language. In M. Lester (ed.) 1970. *Readings in Applied Transformational Grammar.* New York: Holt, Rinehart and Winston.

Newmark, L. and **D. Reibel.** 1968. Necessity and Sufficiency in Language Learning. In M. Lester (ed.) 1970. *Readings in Applied Transformational Grammar.* New York: Holt, Rinehart and Winston.

Nunan, D. 1989. *Designing Tasks for the Communicative Classroom.* Cambridge: Cambridge University Press.

Quirk, R. *et al.* 1985. *A comprehensive Grammar of the English Language.* Harlow: Longman.

Ravem, R. 1974. The development of Wh- questions in first and second language learners. In J. Richards (ed.) 1974. *Error Analysis.* Harlow: Longman.

Rea Dickins, P. M. and **E. G. Woods.** 1988. Some criteria for the development of communicative grammar tasks. TESOL Quarterly, Vol. 22, No. 4.

Richards, J. (ed.) 1984. The status of grammar in the language curriculum. Paper presented at the 19th RELC Seminar.

Richards, J. 1985. *The Context of Language Teaching.* Cambridge: Cambridge University Press.

Richards, J. and **T. Rodgers.** 1986. *Approaches and Methods in Language Teaching.* Cambridge: Cambridge University Press.

Rinvolucri, M. 1984. *Grammar Games.* Cambridge: Cambridge University Press.

Rubin, J. 1975. What the 'good language learner' can teach us. *TESOL Quarterly* Vol. 9, No. 1.

Rutherford, W. 1980. Aspects of pedagogical grammar. *Applied Linguistics* Vol. 1, No. 1.

Selinker, L. 1972. Interlanguage. *IRAL* Vol. 10, No. 3. Heidelberg: Julius Groos Verlag.

References

Sexton, M. and **P. Williams.** 1984. *Communicative Activities for Advanced Students of English.* Munich: Langenscheidt-Longman.

Singleton, D. M. 1981. Age as a factor in second language acquisition. Occasional paper no. 3, Trinity College Dublin, Centre for Language and Communication Studies.

Skehan, P. 1989. *Individual Differences in Second Language Learning.* London: Edward Arnold.

Stubbs, M. 1986. *Educational Linguistics.* Oxford: Basil Blackwell.

Swan, M. and **C. Walter.** 1990. *The New Cambridge English Course.* Cambridge: Cambridge University Press.

Tarone, E. and **G. Yule.** 1989. *Focus on the Learner.* Oxford: Oxford University Press.

Tomlinson, B. 1994. *Openings.* London: Penguin. (First published in London 1986 by Filmscan/Lingual.)

Tongue, R. and **J. Gibbons.** 1982. Structural syllabuses and the young beginner. *Applied Linguistics* Vol. 3, No. 1.

Ur, P. 1988. *Grammar Practice Activities – a practical guide for teachers.* Cambridge: Cambridge University Press.

van Ek, J. 1977. *The Threshold Level for modern Language Learning in Schools.* Harlow: Longman.

van Ek, J. 1986. Objectives for Foreign Language Teaching, Vol. 1. Strasbourg: Council of Europe.

Wakeman, A. 1967. *English Fast.* London: Rupert Hart-Davis.

Widdowson, H. G. 1978. *Teaching Language as Communication.* Oxford: Oxford University Press.

Wilkins, D. 1972. *Linguistics in Language Teaching.* London: Edward Arnold.

Wilkins, D. 1979. Grammatical, situational and notional syllabuses. In C. Brumfit and K. Johnson (eds.) *The Communicative Approach to Language Teaching.* Oxford: Oxford University Press.

Willis, D. 1990. *The Lexical Syllabus.* London: Collins.

Willis, D. and **J. Willis.** 1987. Varied activities for variable language. *ELT Journal* Vol. 41, No. 1.

Willis, D. and **J. Willis.** 1988. *Collins COBUILD English Course.* London: Collins.

Woods, E. G. and **N. J. McLeod.** 1990. *Using English Grammar – meaning and form.* Hemel Hempstead: Prentice Hall.

Woods, E. G. and **N. J. McLeod.** 1992. *Using English Grammar – form and function.* Hemel Hempstead: Prentice Hall.

Wright, T. 1994. *Investigating English.* London: Edward Arnold.

Wright, T. and **R. Bolitho.** 1993. Language Awareness – a missing link in language teacher education? *ELT Journal* Vol. 47, No. 4.

Yalden, J. 1983. *The Communicative Syllabus – evolution, design and implementation.* Oxford: Pergamon Press.

Index

123

Index

Harmer   4, 119
Hartley   52, 119
Hawkins   106, 119
Hoogenraad   119
Hornby   63
Huddleston   3, 119
Hudson   3, 4, 119
Hymes   23, 25, 34, 119

ideology   110
inductive   67, 74, 76–78
information   4, 17
  v. message   27, 29
interlanguage   56, 115
interpretation   19

James   106, 119
Johnson   35, 80, 119
Johnston   36, 119

Krashen   35, 119
Kress   106

language
  child v. adult   55
  Creole   55
  formal/informal   19, 55
  language awareness   57, 59,
    106–112
  Pidgin   55
  psychological   17
  S–O–V   7
  spoken   19
  S–V–O   7, 9, 12, 110
  usage   22, 46, 116
  use   9, 34, 46, 116
    functional use   45
    v. rules   98
  V–S–O   7
  written   19

Larsen-Freeman   42–43, 54, 119
learner
  age   41, 66, 72
  centredness   78–81
  classroom   80
  field-dependent   72
  field-independent   72
  learning experience   66, 73
  personality   66, 72
  variables   65–66
learning
  pragmatic mode   55
  strategies   52
  syntactic mode   55
Leech   2, 18, 21, 24, 113, 119
lexical item   18
linguistic competence   26
little   5
  least   6
  less   6
Littlejohn et al.   78, 119
Littlewood   27, 119

McLeod   91, 94, 95, 98, 99, 100,
    102, 103, 109, 121
Malcolm, Derek   108
message   11, 31
  v. information   27, 29
method
  audio-lingual   63–64
  direct   62
  grammar-translation   62
  natural   62
  oral approach   62–63
methodology   61
  interactive   71–74
modals   85, 104, 109
morpheme   40, 116
morphology   2, 3
Murphy   84, 85, 117

Index